Greater Than

Discovering the Things That Keep Us from God's Best

Tim Ingram

renownpublishing

Renown Publishing
www.renownpublishing.com

Greater Than / Tim Ingram
ISBN-13: 978-1-952602-63-4

To my incredible wife and best friend, Tina—I wouldn't be here without you. The encouragement, love, and kindness you have given me has changed the course of my life forever. I am who I am because you have always believed in me. Thank you for being by my side through thick and thin, good times and bad, always loving, supporting, and praying for me. You are my hero.

To my amazing son, TJ—there has never been a day when I haven't been in awe of the amazing young man you are. Your passion, talents, and giftings are world-class, and I am so incredibly proud to be your dad. Don't ever quit.

To my beautiful daughter, Natalie—I cannot imagine my life without you. The world is a better place because you are in it. You are a powerful, unique, and amazing daughter of God, and I believe that you can do anything you set your mind to.

CONTENTS

Willie Robertson

I know there are times in my life when I have put things above God without realizing it. We can idolize success, money, and the good ole days. Pastor Tim Ingram's book is a great breakdown of the lies we can believe over God's word. God is "Greater Than" anything we have walked through, labels that have been put on us, our failures, and times when we feel we don't have enough. *Greater Than* takes a practical look at how to overcome these idols and shares Tim's personal journey to discovering that God can overcome any of these. You will be reminded that God's word is still true today and always will be.

I have seen this in my own family. The Robertsons have received so much more from God than we could have ever done on our own. In fact, without Jesus, we would not even have stayed together as a family. It hasn't always been easy, and we have had struggles, issues, and pains from the past, but God is always in control! He had a beautiful plan for us and has plans for you. This book will help you to discover even more that you belong to him!

I love Tim's humor, experiences, and perspective that illustrates how we serve a God who we can do way more with than we can do on our own. But, we have to trust him! We have to take faith steps, get rid of our idols in our heart, and discover the purpose he has for us. I highly recommend this book for anyone who is wanting to grow in their faith and trust God with their future! Thank you, Tim, for putting this down on paper to help us overcome the schemes of the evil one and trust more in God.

—Willie Robertson

TIM INGRAM

Introduction

I know that the LORD is great, that our Lord is greater than all gods.

—Psalm 135:5 *(NIV)*

Let's begin with a disclaimer. I'm not the world's leader in spiritual things, smart ideas, or practical help. I don't have awards, degrees, or many accolades. I don't have much that would make my life special or unique in any way—except for one thing: I have made a choice to surrender my life completely to Jesus Christ.

That's it.

He is what makes me worthy, and He can do the same for you. His love found me at my lowest and invited me to love Him in return. His grace overwhelmed me and compels me to help as many people as possible in the time He has given me. His friendship has patiently called me out of my sin and into a life that I couldn't have dreamed of having. He has shown me my purpose: to help people know Him better.

In order for us to know Him better, there has to be a letting go of things that we have inadvertently allowed to take His place, things that we believe are somehow greater than He is. We may not realize how influential these things can be, but they hold incredible power over us and keep us from becoming all that He wants us to be. These things are false gods—insufficient, worthless replicas that have robbed God's people of a true relationship with Him for thousands of years.

From the beginning of time, mankind has worshiped things that are worthless. People have devoted their lives to foolish things that cannot possibly measure up to expectations. Time and time again, men and women have been left disappointed, unfulfilled, and wondering why their prayers are unanswered. I believe that many people today are still worshiping idols.

When we think of idols, or false gods, it's easy for us to dismiss idolatry as a thing of the ancient past. Long gone are the days of bowing down to some golden snake or half-naked man-fish—or are they?

Today's idol worship takes on many complicated forms, which we must acknowledge honestly and turn from in order to recognize the greatness and wonder of the one true God. An idol is anything we consider more fundamental than God for our joy, identity, self-worth, or security.

God wants you to know Him truly and intimately. He wants to connect with you and show you His power. In order to connect with the real God, you have to let go of the twisted illusions you have unknowingly put your hope in.

When we cling to our idols, which are pathetic in comparison to God, it reminds me of a story I once heard about a woman who traveled to a foreign country. On her way home, she spotted the cutest little puppy she had ever seen. Knowing that she would probably be stopped at customs, she carefully placed the puppy into her large handbag and smuggled it into the U.S.

Upon her arrival home, she placed the puppy into the care of her other, larger dogs. However, the other dogs didn't take to this puppy, so she brought it into her own bed and decided to cuddle this puppy and show it lots of love. Soon, however, her other dogs became ill. Being a caring person, she marched her crew of dogs off to the vet. The vet inspected all of the dogs and came out of the examination room a short time later to ask the woman where she had obtained her new puppy. The woman had no choice but to confess that she had smuggled it into the country illegally.

The veterinarian nodded. "Well, this situation makes sense now because that puppy is no puppy. You smuggled in a foreign rat!"

Of course, the woman was completely shocked and upset that she had been hiding and clinging to something that wasn't worthy of her love, affection, and attention. This creature was something that had no place living inside her home, let alone winning the affections of her heart. Not only that, but this object of misplaced affection had hurt those she loved, her dogs.

While this story may seem shocking to some, haven't we all done the same thing this poor woman did? We smuggle into our hearts our addictions, desires, insecurities, sinful habits, and hurts.

Every day, I encounter people of all ages and religious backgrounds who are cuddled up to their rats of choice rather than God. They're confused about who God is. Some are mad at Him, frustrated with what they believe is His unwillingness to help them. They blame the real God for not answering prayers they have offered to something else. Desperation, burnout, and disappointment are quick to follow when our false gods show how powerless they are.

Trusting in the Lord requires knowing Him and being close to Him. He will speak directly to you when you share an intimate personal relationship with Him. He will meet you where you are if you are truly looking for Him.

An honest look at modern-day idolatry and an acceptance of how I've been deceived has led me to a relationship with God that is greater than anything I could have imagined. He is real. He is amazing. He loves me, and I know that He loves you, too.

In this book, we'll begin the process of uncovering who the real God is while exposing what we have settled for instead. We'll name these false gods and discover how easy it is for us to be deceived by them. As we expose and deal with modern-day idols, I'll share some of my story and invite you to make a decision to allow the Holy Spirit to help you deal with your issues as well. Step by step, we will turn away from foolish idols and embrace a God who is truly *Greater Than* all!

CHAPTER ONE

Greater Than M.E.
(My Ego)

When my wife and I first met, I was dumbstruck by her beautiful smile. There was an immediate attraction, and I couldn't wait to ask her out on a date. It took some getting over my nerves, but when she finally saw the light and agreed to meet me for coffee, we had a fantastic first date and an amazingly honest discussion.

Our conversation began with the usual get-to-know-you banter but then quickly led to a more serious discussion of what each of us was looking for in a relationship. We were honest and clear about what we couldn't tolerate and what we were believing God for. We both had issues that were very near and dear to our hearts, and we agreed that being transparent and direct with each other was the kindest thing to do. This kept us from wasting each other's time and helped us to avoid many arguments later on as the relationship progressed.

We called this our Define the Relationship, or DTR, moment. That first conversation set us up for more success than we could ever have imagined at the time. We got on the same page from the beginning and have been walking in unity ever since.

All healthy relationships should have a Define the Relationship moment. God had a DTR moment with the Israelites in Exodus 20 when He gave them the Ten Commandments. The first four commandments address our relationship with God and our hearts toward Him. The rest deal with how we should treat other people. Jesus summed up the Ten Commandments and boiled them down to two: "'Love the Lord your God with all your heart and with all your soul and with all your mind.' This is the first and greatest commandment. And the second is like it: 'Love your neighbor as yourself.' All the Law and the Prophets hang on these two commandments" (Matthew 22:37–40 NIV).

Let's talk about what God meant when He commanded us to love Him:

> *You shall have no other gods before me. You shall not make for yourself an image in the form of anything in heaven above or on the earth beneath or in the waters below. You shall not bow down to them or worship them; for I, the LORD your God, am a jealous God, punishing the children for the sin of the parents to the third and fourth generation of those who hate me, but showing love to a thousand generations of those who love me and keep my commandments.*
> *—Exodus 20:3–6 (NIV)*

A jealous God? Isn't that bad? No! God's jealousy means that He longs for you. He wants your worship to be devoted to Him and Him alone. When you turn your attention to things other than Him, He says, "You belong to Me! We're in a relationship here. When you run after other things, I get jealous!"

It's easy for us to look at this and think that it's manipulative, but that depends on the filter you're using. If you understand God's commandments through His amazing love, then you'll understand that following them is how you love Him.

Prior to Exodus 20, God led His people out of slavery (Exodus 3–15). In Exodus 20, He was preparing to take them into the promised land, but before they entered it, He needed to have a DTR moment with them.

In this scripture, God laid out what He was looking for from us and communicated everything He expects, but we must be honest with Him and ourselves in return. Do we really want Him *fully* in and over our lives, or do we just want the occasional blessing or answered prayer? God is not a genie who exists only to grant each and every one of our wishes. He is our Creator, Lord, and Savior, and He deserves our worship.

Just as we have expectations regarding our close relationships, so does God.

God wants us to be faithful to Him. What or whom we worship matters. God doesn't want our hearts to betray Him by committing adultery with other gods.

The Idol of M.E. (My Ego)

I believe the greatest contender against God being first in our lives is our own ego. Nothing will keep us from worshiping God alone and honoring the first commandment like our worship of self—the idol of M.E.

We tend to fall into the trap of letting our own ego rule our lives. We look at the things we accomplish and think, "Look at what I've done!" We consider ourselves to be the most important aspect of our own lives.

Pride is what removed the devil from heaven (Isaiah 14:12–15). In fact, when pride rose up in his heart, he was immediately cast out of heaven. God will not tolerate pride, but we still tend to make an idol out of it. When we set our hearts on ourselves, we bypass what God has said in His Word and set up our own little kingdoms. If we don't get our pride in check, nothing else in this book will matter. God is greater than M.E.! He is greater than my desires, stresses, anxieties, and fears. He is greater than all other gods, including my ego.

Daniel 4 tells us a story about King Nebuchadnezzar, who was warned about his pride. Even though God warned him, he decided not to listen. He continued to hold on to his pride, as many of us do. He looked across his kingdom and thought, "Look at what I've done. Look how awesome my work is!" The consequences came immediately, and he lost his mind. All of his subjects saw him go crazy. He took off his clothes, started acting nuts, and ended up getting banished. This king went from being on top of the world to becoming an outcast.

The good news is that God didn't leave Nebuchadnez-zar in this state. Daniel 4:34 says, "I, Nebuchadnezzar, raised my eyes toward heaven, and my sanity was restored. Then I praised the Most High; I honored and glorified him who lives forever" (NIV). When Nebuchadnezzar worshiped God with a humble heart, God renewed his mind and restored him to his place as king. This was his DTR moment.

Pride isn't something that only rulers of great kingdoms need to guard themselves against. I remember a moment of pride I had as a kid growing up in Texas. In west Texas, there are two religions: Christianity and foot-ball—and we don't joke about either one. In the late '80s, Permian High School in Odessa, Texas, was a legendary football powerhouse known all over the nation. The movie and TV show *Friday Night Lights* feature Permian High School and their legendary football team. Their players were revered throughout the state. Easily recognized by their black-and-white letterman jackets, they brought a sense of awe anytime they were spotted in public.

The apartment complex that my family lived in had a common area, and we loved to play football there every Saturday morning, pretending to be these legends. We spent hours in the hot sun, imitating every single move they had made the Friday night before. One Saturday, our dreams became a reality when two Permian players spot-ted us playing football and asked to join the game. We were speechless in their presence. These were our heroes. The only response I could think of was: "Absolutely, as long as I'm on your team!"

We spent the rest of the day dominating every kid in the apartment complex. When I say "we," I mean the Permian players, but I was on their team. It was a moment I will never forget. For once, I was on the winning side! For a few moments in time, my dream of playing with my heroes came true, and I would never let my apartment friends forget "our" domination.

This story may seem harmless. You probably have your own story of pride you've taken in an accomplishment or opportunity. What we need to understand is that pride is the human way, but it's not God's way. God has warned His people, time and time again, that He does not tolerate pride. Pride means that we're putting ourselves in the position of god when there is only one true God.

James 4:6 says that "God resists the proud, but gives grace to the humble" (GNT). The word *resist* in the biblical Greek means "to play on the other team."[1] Think about this. When you live in pride, God is playing against you. It's because of your pride that He resists you. On the other hand, when you humble yourself and find grace, you find covering for your sin and empowerment to rise up.

> *Now I, Nebuchadnezzar, praise and exalt and glorify the King of heaven, because everything he does is right and all his ways are just. And those who walk in pride he is able to humble.*
>
> **—Daniel 4:37** *(NIV)*

Proverbs 16:18 says, "Pride goes before destruction, a haughty spirit before a fall" (NIV). Nebuchadnezzar learned this the hard way. He lost everything. The good news is that the blessings of humble worship far outweigh the consequences of our pride.

Worship Matters

In Exodus 20, God told His people that He wanted to be worshiped first in their lives. Idol worship isn't something to be trifled with. It's not cute or funny to devote your heart to someone or something other than God. Worshiping idols is committing adultery against God! It's betrayal, and it hurts His heart. There are four reasons why worshiping God alone matters to Him and why we should ensure that we fix our worship on the correct Person.

Worship Is Why We Were Created

Revelation 4:11 says, "Worthy are you, our Lord and God, to receive glory and honor and power, for you created all things, and by your will they existed and were created" (ESV). Everything was created to bring Him glory. The Word tells us, "The heavens declare the glory of God; the skies proclaim the work of his hands" (Psalm 19:1 NIV). Isaiah 55:12 says that "all the trees of the field will clap their hands" (NIV).

Creation is glorifying God! It's one of the reasons we feel connected to God when we sit in nature. If you're like me, you sit in a deer blind, waiting for something to come out that you can slay and eat. Maybe you feel most connected to God when you're sitting on a beach, listening to the waves crash against the shore and feeling the warmth of the sun on your skin. Perhaps you enjoy the vast expanse of a mountaintop view. In those moments, you feel close to God because the divine Creator is connecting with His creation.

Not only is nature constantly bringing glory to God, but it's in our genetics to bring Him praise as well. Isaiah 43:20–21 says, "The wild animals honor me, the jackals and the owls, because I provide water in the wilderness and streams in the wasteland, to give drink to my people, my chosen, the people I formed for myself that they may proclaim my praise" (NIV). God's greatest desire for you is that you would use your life to bring Him praise. We all exist to bring glory to God.

The enemy will do everything in His power to keep you from discovering this simple purpose for your life. If you're not careful, you'll spend your life worshiping things that don't matter. It frustrates God when His people worship worthless idols. Time and time again, we break the heart of our Father and turn our own hearts to things that do nothing for us in return!

Think about how many times we defend people who don't even know that we exist. We might defend our favorite sports teams, but they don't know us or care about us. If we're so willing to give our devotion to people who don't even know or value us, how much more should we devote ourselves to the One who created us, chooses us, and wants us? We are to be devoted to God alone, period.

When we embrace the fact that we were created to worship God, we begin to discover our true purpose, which is to bring Him glory and honor in response to His great love for us. However, it's easy for us to get distracted and miss God's plan if we don't stop and listen to what He is saying to us and what He wants for us. When we're self-focused in our interactions with God, it's like going out on a first date with someone who can't stop talking about himself or herself. We come to God in prayer, and the topic of conversation is me, me, me. We need to turn off our thoughts and wants and be quiet for a change. We need to stop and listen. If we don't learn to focus on God, we'll end up worshiping things that do not and cannot possibly love us back.

Worship Is a Sacred Choice

Worship isn't worship if it's forced, the same way love isn't love if it's forced. God is a gentleman. He is never going to make you worship Him. Even though it's your purpose, He gives you a choice. Worship is a declaration of your love and admiration. It will bring about wonderful things for you when you worship the One you're meant to worship.

In Exodus 20:5, the word translated as *worship* is the Hebrew word *'ābaḏ*, which means "to be a slave to, to be forced into labor for."[2] When you worship idols, it puts you back into bondage. The Bible says, "It is for freedom that Christ has set us free" (Galatians 5:1 NIV). God sets His children free, but when we worship idols, we go right back into slavery (Romans 8:14–17; Galatians 5:1).

Worship Has Blessings and Consequences

We're free to make choices, but we're not free to avoid consequences. There's a high price to pay for low living.

There's a price to pay for idol worship. God is very clear: there's no excuse when we bypass His ways. He wants us to know that worshiping things other than Him brings consequences.

In Deuteronomy 30, God brought His people right to the edge of the promised land, and He began to talk to them about what they were going to face:

> *See, I have set before you today life and good, death and evil. If you obey the commandments of the LORD your God that I command you today, by loving the LORD your God, by walking in his ways, and by keeping his commandments and his statutes and his rules, then you shall live and multiply, and the LORD your God will bless you in the land that you are entering to take possession of it. But if your heart turns away, and you will not hear, but are drawn away to worship other gods and serve them, I declare to you today, that you shall surely perish. You shall not live long in the land that you are going over the Jordan to enter and possess. I call heaven and earth to witness against you today, that I have set before you life and death, blessing and curse. Therefore choose life, that you and your offspring may live, loving the LORD your God, obeying his voice and holding fast to him, for he is your life and length of days, that you may dwell in the land that the LORD swore to your fathers, to Abraham, to Isaac, and to Jacob, to give them.*
> *—Deuteronomy 30:15–20 (ESV)*

If you love and honor God, you'll be blessed. Life is an open-book test, and He is giving you the answers in His Word. This is a great picture of the heart of a good father. Because God is a good Father, He is telling us there are consequences for playing in the street or running into traffic.

True Worship Makes Us Humble

God gave up His one and only Son *for you.* Your punishment was laid upon Him. When you grasp the power of the cross, there's a new humility that comes to you. It's the gut-punch your ego needs. When you recognize that you deserve to be on the cross, but He took your place, your only response is to worship Him in humility.

It's time to get honest and question ourselves. In John 5, Jesus asked the paralytic man if he wanted to get well. The man responded with excuses for why he couldn't get well. Ask yourself the same question Jesus asked him: "Do you want to get well?" (John 5:6 NIV). Do you want to overcome the sins that constantly dog you? Do you want to overcome anxiety, depression, and the pressure to keep up appearances and stay in step with the folks next door?

Maybe you don't know what you want. Well, there's an easy way to find out. We know what we want based on where we spend our time and energy. Real growth and change happen when our wants and desires meet up with God's. That's what is known as a match made in heaven.

True worship begins at the cross when we recognize that God, in His amazing love, took the punishment we deserved and put it on His Son. The Bible says that "God demonstrates his own love for us in this: While we were still sinners, Christ died for us" (Romans 5:8 NIV). When we truly understand this, we can't help but respond by loving God in return, walking with Him in humility, and giving Him His rightful place as first in our hearts.

REFLECTION

Chapter One Prompt

Holy Spirit, what are You saying to me?

_____

_____

_____

_____

_____

_____

_____

_____

_____

_____

_____

_____

_____

_____

Holy Spirit, what step(s) do You want me to take?

_____

_____

_____

_____

_____

_____

_____

_____

_____

_____

_____

_____

_____

_____

_____

_____

_____

_____

_____

_____

CHAPTER TWO

Greater Than G.O.D.S.
(Good Old Days Syndrome)

We all love to see transformation. We're drawn to movies and shows that capture stories of people's lives going from pathetic to awe-inspiring, and we like to root for the underdog in sports. I think it's because there's a little bit of God's heart reflected in those kinds of experiences.

My grandmother was fighting dementia at the end of her life, and I would sometimes sit with her and watch reruns of sports clips of her favorite team, the Dallas Cowboys. As a lifelong fan, her eyes lit up, even in her weakened mental state, every time she heard her team mentioned. She had been devastated by the firing of legendary coach Tom Landry when it happened in 1989. Twenty years later, this news was completely new to her once again, and her pain was as real as it had been two decades earlier. She began to scream at the TV, "Oh my gosh, what is wrong with them? They will never win another game!"

I said, "Grandma, they've won three Super Bowls since then!" I got to share the story of the Cowboys' miraculous redemption, and we reveled in the good ol' days as I told her about the victories like it was her first time hearing it. Then she said, "I guess things turned out okay then!"

God, too, loves a good redemption story. He loves to give us redemption in place of all the junk we have in our lives. If we want God to redeem and transform our lives, it's important that we release our yesterdays and let Him deal with the things we're holding on to in unhealthy ways. Let me just say it: Hey, Cowboys fans, maybe it's time we let go of the past, too!

Idolizing our past is what I like to call the "Good Ol' Days Syndrome" (G.O.D.S.). We often make an idol out of our past. Remember Psalm 135:5 from the introduction: "I know that the LORD is great, that our Lord is greater than all gods" (NIV). As we confront the idol of the past, let's revisit what an idol is. An idol is anything we draw from other than God for our joy, our identity, our self-worth, or our security. It's anything that we place above God and consider more important than He is.

Of course, this is a problem, but it's so common for human beings to do this that it's difficult for us to recognize. It's a timeless issue—not just in the Old Testament and New Testament, but throughout history and even today. It's difficult to see ourselves as idol worshipers, but many of us are. God wants to expose those things and deal with them.

As usual, the children of Israel made a great example:

They rejected his decrees and the covenant he had made
with their ancestors and the statutes he had warned them
to keep. They followed worthless idols and themselves be-
came worthless. They imitated the nations around them
although the LORD had ordered them, "Do not do as they
do."

—2 Kings 17:15 *(NIV)*

I want you to see this. The people of Israel worshiped God, but they also "followed worthless idols" as they "imitated the nations around them." We do the exact same thing today! We worship the Lord, but we have other things in our lives that are customary, other things that take our worship, adoration, and affection.

God told the Israelites, "Look, I'm putting you in a timeout!" In this case, the timeout was exile. He told them that He was taking them out of the land He had promised them. They forfeited His blessings when they chose to become like the nations around them instead of listening to God and following His instructions.

Verse 15 says that the people of Israel became worthless because they worshiped worthless things. These idols don't give us grace; they don't provide for us. The more we value and worship things that can't love us back, the more we become like them. The people of Israel imitated the nations around them even though God had told them not to, and as a result, they lost out on His blessings.

God calls us to a different path! He is calling us to allow Him onto the throne of our hearts in place of our yesterdays. It can be very easy to hold on to things of the past, because we've become accustomed to it. The more we hold on to these things, the worse it gets. But God is greater than our past!

When we worship the wrong things, we devalue the things that are priceless. We don't treat this like the big deal that it is. We may not even notice it—that is, until it starts affecting our children and our grandchildren. You can be sure of this: if you hold on to your yesterdays, you're not the only one it's affecting. You will actually begin building a generational stronghold for your children and grandchildren, passing it on from one generation to the next. Look at how this plays out in 2 Kings 17:40–41 (NIV):

> They would not listen, however, but persisted in their former practices. Even while these people were worshiping the LORD, they were serving their idols. To this day their children and grandchildren continue to do as their ancestors did.

That's called a generational curse! God wants to be Lord of *all*, not Lord of *most*, and certainly not Lord of *some*. Let's back up a bit. Second Kings 17:7 says, "All this took place because the Israelites had sinned against the LORD their God, who had brought them up out of Egypt from under the power of Pharaoh king of Egypt. They worshiped other gods..." (NIV). That's where it all began—way back in Egypt.

As a professional communicator, I've worked hard to overcome my Texas twang in order to connect with people better, but every once in a while, I recognize that funny look when I say "y'all," "ain't," or "bless your heart."

Texas twang is a hard habit to break. You can take the person out of the country, but you can't take the country out of the person.

We can struggle to change in our Christian lives as well. Sometimes God wants to deliver us out of something, but we stay stuck in the bad habits and the sin nature of our past. That means we're refusing to let God be the Lord of those areas of our hearts. We become accustomed to them, baby them, and make provision for them. We actually like them, so we begin to think that they're valuable to us. Meanwhile, God is begging us to try His way. He is greater than our hurts, our fears, our wins, and our losses. Our God is greater than our yesterdays!

God brought His people out of Egypt, and many times after that, He delivered them from other nations. Despite this, the people of Israel picked up idols from those other nations and worshiped them. In 2 King 17, God was saying, "You know what, that's it! I have shown you what it's like to be My favorite and experience My blessings. I have shown you something so much better, yet you keep choosing something else, something that's so much less than who you really are. You're better than this!"

Three Ways We Make Idols of Our Past

Your past cannot determine your future. It only gives God a good place to start. What could God do if you were to give Him the past and ask Him to start with that?

The past is a launching pad; it's not a place to return to. You can't live life always looking in the rearview mirror. So, what does it look like to worship the good ol' days? Let's take an honest look at ourselves in light of the three ways we make idols of our past.

The Idol of Our Wins

In theological terms, we call this Uncle Rico Syndrome. If you've ever watched *Napoleon Dynamite*, you know that Uncle Rico is a guy who is always living in the past.[3] He looks back and thinks about how great he was, at least in his own mind. You know, nothing is more pathetic than the guy thirty years out of high school who still talks about how amazing an athlete he was and how he would have gone pro if it weren't for this or that.

Sometimes we get so lost in thinking about all the great things we did thirty years ago that we forget to see how great God is in our lives today. God has a future and a hope for you (Jeremiah 29:11). He wants to redeem all of our days, not just our yesterdays. God has great things in store for His people if we are willing to give Him our wins. The good ol' days aren't a bad thing unless they cause us to stop believing God for fresh things today.

One of my favorite things about being a pastor is seeing the culture that has been developed in my church. At the beginning of every church service, we celebrate a win. We find things that God is doing, make them big, and praise God for them. We honor Him for changing lives and for the breakthroughs He brings. We take note of these things, and then we leave them there and set new goals.

It's one thing to celebrate a win and another thing to be always looking back at that moment. God has great things He still wants to do. If you're not dead, He is not done!

Ecclesiastes 7:10 tells us, "Say not, 'Why were the former days better than these?' For it is not from wisdom that you ask this" (ESV). It's not wise to live in the past.

All too often, we see life as a highlight reel. We recall the highlights but forget about the problems or consequences from yesterday. I mean, let's be honest—it wasn't that great! It came with a price tag. Some of those wins were hard-fought.

It's kind of like social media. You only see the things that people want you to see. Similarly, your yesterdays are only the things that you allow yourself to remember.

This reminds me of the Israelites in Exodus 14:10–12. They saw that Pharaoh was coming after them, and fear gripped their hearts. They started complaining to Moses, "Hey, wouldn't we be better off if you had left us in Egypt?"

Hold the phone. What happened in Egypt? They were slaves in Egypt! Boy, hearts can be fickle. They weren't thinking about the fact that they had been delivered from slavery. They were dwelling on the fact that they had at least known what to expect in Egypt. They were thinking, "We had value and purpose there. Even though we were the lowest man on the totem pole, we were still on the totem pole, right?" In Exodus 14:12, they said, "Didn't we say to you in Egypt, 'Leave us alone; let us serve the Egyptians'? It would have been better for us to serve the Egyptians than to die in the desert!" (NIV).

The Israelites were stuck in the moment and didn't realize where God was leading them. Sometimes we quit in the middle of something because we find ourselves in a circumstance that's not ideal. We want to walk our way back into slavery because it's comfortable. We fall back into our habits because they're all we know. God deserves more than this from us. He is greater than the good ol' days!

When new believers encounter spiritual warfare, they may be tempted to give up. It's easy to fall back into old mindsets and old habits. Reaching a better future requires us to trust God with that next step.

In Exodus, the people of Israel didn't realize that they would someday become a world superpower with nuclear weapons. What is Egypt today? Nothing compared to the progress Israel has made. They have pyramids and some camels, but their best years are behind them. God had a special future planned for Israel.

As He did for Israel, God has a future for you and a future for your children. However, you must be willing to surrender your wins, because they aren't that great compared to the greatness of your God.

Deuteronomy 1:30 says that God goes before you. The past looks good to us because we know that when there were struggles, it eventually worked out, right? Well, when we look at the present, it seems like we don't have those guarantees. However, we do have God's promise that He goes before us: "The LORD himself goes before you and will be with you; he will never leave you nor forsake you" (Deuteronomy 31:8 NIV). This is a promise from God, but you have to be willing to move for God and let go of the wins of yesterday.

The Idol of Shoulda, Coulda, Woulda

I'm not going to lie—sometimes I get caught up in the idol of "shoulda, coulda, woulda." I've thought, "Oh, if only I would've invested in Apple! I had a hunch that they were going to be a big thing. If only I had invested all our money, I'd be a billionaire now!" For you, it might have been the loss of a person, a job, a marriage, a friendship, or an opportunity.

These losses can leave us stuck and believing that God didn't come through for us. We build tombstones and monuments to our past, and we sit next to them, dreaming about days that never really happened. We think, "What would life have been like if I had just done X, Y, Z?" We replay it over and over and over in our minds.

There's a time to grieve, but we can't stay there, my friend. It's not healthy! In Matthew 5:4, Jesus said, "Blessed are those who mourn, for they will be comforted" (NIV). There's a time to mourn, but there's also a time to let Him comfort you and call you out of the losses of your past. Grieving should not last forever. You've got to move on.

We can thank God for the memories we have and the opportunities we've had. Then we can look forward to the opportunities that are to come. You're still alive, so keep going! Loss and grief are difficult things, but you aren't to build an idol out of them. Allow God to be greater than your grief, even when it hurts.

The Idol of Our Experiences with God

Some people like to make their experiences the end-all, be-all in life. These are the old-time religious people who say, "I'm the King James Version-only person because that's what Jesus read," or "If you have anything other than a piano in the church, it's demonic."

I saw a sign on a church one time that said, "We're King James Version only. We don't change the Bible. The Bible changes us." I thought, "Take it easy! We're not changing the Bible. Nobody reads old English, not even you!" Let me give you a nickel's worth of free advice: in case you didn't know, Jesus didn't speak old English.

Let's be real and admit that we all make idols out of our experiences with God. We only experience a third of His greatness when we choose to limit ourselves to only what we've known through our own experiences. Many times, we go just far enough with God and then we limit Him, thinking that He can't do anything beyond our imaginations. This makes for a small God!

God operates outside of our human minds. He can do whatever He wants, any time He wants. He is way beyond what we can understand.

When we make idols out of our experiences with God, we limit Him. The Jews had this problem, too. They refused to accept the Gentiles in the New Testament. It was such a point of contention that even Paul and Peter, two amazing followers of Christ, got into a massive argument over it (Galatians 2).

Paul confronted Peter, telling him that he was wrong. Peter was saying, "This is just for the Jews. These Gentiles don't follow our ways. God can't move in them!"

Paul came back with: "You're out of your mind! God has us moving in a new direction."

On a different occasion, God gave Peter a dream, showing him that He poured out His Spirit on *all* people (Acts 10). Peter needed to understand that God was doing a new thing. It's okay for God to do new things. You don't have to understand something for it to be God's will and His work.

Jesus dealt with this as well. In Matthew 13:54, Jesus went to His hometown and began teaching people. The people were amazed, but not in a good way:

> *"Where did this man get this wisdom and these miraculous powers?" they asked. "Isn't this the carpenter's son? Isn't his mother's name Mary, and aren't his brothers James, Joseph, Simon and Judas? Aren't all his sisters with us? Where then did this man get all these things?" And they took offense at him.*
> **—Matthew 13:54–57** *(NIV)*

They were saying, "We saw Jesus grow up! I know His family. This isn't right." They were limiting the power of God by refusing to see that He was right in front of them. They were offended.

God wants to deal with our yesterdays, but instead of receiving His miracles, sometimes we take offense. We say, "How dare You, God! This defines me! I want to hold on to this." How did Jesus respond when that happened? He said, "A prophet is not without honor except in his own town and in his own home" (Matthew 13:57 NIV). People received Jesus' message everywhere He went except in

His own hometown, where they limited Him because of their experience with Him in the past.

God doesn't put limits on you because of your past. When He looks at you, He sees potential. If you let Him deal with your yesterdays, your future can be amazing! What happened with the unbelieving people in Jesus' hometown? Matthew 13:58 says that Jesus "did not do many miracles there because of their lack of faith" (NIV). This is a faith issue. Limiting God to only what we can understand severely weakens our faith and keeps us from seeing Him move today.

Give God your yesterdays. The good ol' days aren't better, so let go of them. God is saying to you, "Remember not the former things, nor consider the things of old. Behold, I am doing a new thing; now it springs forth, do you not perceive it?" (Isaiah 43:18–19 ESV). Don't you see it? Don't you feel it? God wants to do a new thing in your heart!

REFLECTION

Chapter Two Prompt

Holy Spirit, what are You saying to me?

_____

_____

_____

_____

_____

_____

_____

_____

_____

_____

_____

_____

_____

_____

Holy Spirit, what step(s) do You want me to take?

_____

_____

_____

_____

_____

_____

_____

_____

_____

_____

_____

_____

_____

_____

_____

_____

_____

_____

_____

CHAPTER THREE

Greater Than F.O.P.O.
(Fear of People's Opinions)

When my son was in elementary school, we started having major issues with the way he was treating other students. Parenting him was proving to be a challenge, as he was constantly getting into trouble at school. On one particular day, his teacher contacted me to let me know that my son had written a very bad word on the notebook of another student, shocking and upsetting her. My son, being a pastor's kid, knew that bad words and hurting others were a big deal in our family. When he came home that day, he knew beyond the shadow of a doubt that punishment was guaranteed to follow.

I rarely used spanking as a way to discipline my kids, but this was one of those occasions when it was called for because my son needed to understand the impact of his actions. My son slowly walked upstairs to his room, and I said, "Let's talk." We discussed what he had done, and he acted remorseful about his behavior, but I didn't know how genuine his remorse was.

In my heart, I began to pray, "Lord, help me. I'm at my wit's end with this kid. Would You show me how to get through to him somehow?" At that moment, I felt the Lord leading me to do something I'd never done before. I looked at my son and said, "You know I promised you that the next time you hurt another student, it was going to result in a spanking. Do you remember when we talked about that?"

"Yes," he agreed.

Then I asked him, "Do you think you deserve a spanking?"

"Yes." He started crying.

I couldn't hold back the tears welling up in my own eyes. "Son, you know that you deserve a spanking. Now I'm going to show you what grace is."

He looked up at me, puzzled. "What do you mean?"

"There's a difference between grace and mercy. Grace is getting what you don't deserve, and mercy is not getting what you deserve. So today, instead of you getting a spanking, which you admitted that you deserve, I'm going to take your spanking for you." Then I handed the belt to him, laid across the bed, and watched the shock and awe in his face as the tables were suddenly reversed.

He didn't end up spanking me, of course. He just couldn't do it. But it was a powerful moment when things began to change in his heart. Now he had a new understanding of what grace truly looked like.

Any parent who takes great joy in disciplining their children is probably abusive. On the other hand, good parents discipline their children because they want to recapture their hearts and help them to come back to what they know is right. This is how God speaks to His children today.

In the previous chapter, I mentioned that God was going to send His people into exile because of their idol worship. Well, in Ezekiel 14, His people were in exile in Babylon. The leaders came to the prophet Ezekiel, looking for a word from God. They wanted to know how long they were going to be in exile.

While Ezekiel sat with the elders of Israel, a message came to him from God: "Son of man, these leaders have set up idols in their hearts. They have embraced things that will make them fall into sin" (Ezekiel 14:1–3 NLT). Notice that the idols God spoke of weren't in their homes or temples; the idols were in their hearts. God said, "Why should I listen to their requests?" (Ezekiel 14:3 NLT). These people obviously didn't love God—so why should He listen to their questions? These were stern words from a stern God.

It matters what you worship. It matters what sits on the throne of your heart. In this passage, God gave the elders of Israel the kind of answer that their great idolatry deserved. It wasn't what they wanted to hear. You may be wondering why God came down so strong on them. If you are, you may be missing the point. God wanted to recapture the hearts and minds of His people, and He wants to recapture our hearts, too.

Those who came to Ezekiel were the leaders of God's people. They should have known better. The people were looking to them for answers. These leaders should've been able to hear from God for themselves. They knew why they were in exile. At that point, God had been begging and warning His people for years, through His prophets, to change their ways. Now they found themselves right in the middle of the consequences. They weren't ignorant. Their questions were out of defiance.

Are parts of your life in defiance of God's Word or His ways? This could keep you from hearing God for yourself. You may know beyond a shadow of a doubt that there are things in your life that don't belong. This is blatant sin!

God does not bless disobedience. He can't. If you're living in disobedience, God is calling you back to Him today. I've often said that when the heart is wrong, the discipline lasts long. When the heart is right, the idol takes flight. If it rhymes, it must be true!

Mark Emmons was an incredible competitive rifle shooter. In the 2004 Olympics, he was on his final shot. All he had to do was hit the target anywhere, and he would win the gold medal. He took a deep breath, fired his rifle, and it hit dead bullseye—on the wrong target! I can't describe the look on his face. Imagine all the years of training, the pursuit of perfection, undone by one mistake![4]

This is a good picture of what sin causes us to do. We aim at the wrong target, and when we do, we hit it every time. Idol worship leads us further and further into sin, but God has something far better in mind for us.

The people in Ezekiel 14 refused to give up their idols. They refused to change, so God essentially said, "You think that your timeout is over? It's just begun!" God's deliverance moves at the speed of our obedience. He wants our hearts and will wait as long as it takes to get them.

Fear of People's Opinions

I believe that the leaders of Israel in Ezekiel 14 had a Fear of People's Opinions (F.O.P.O.). Their appearances, status, and respectability had become their highest priority, which is still true for many of us today. The fear of looking bad or seeming less than perfect makes an idol out of other people's opinions, but we're doing this constantly. This is the next idol we'll address in this book.

A Snare

In 2 Kings 5, we find a man who made F.O.P.O. his idol. He just didn't know any better. This guy was eaten up by the idol of the fear of man.

Proverbs 29:25 says, "Fear of man will prove to be a snare, but whoever trusts in the LORD is kept safe" (NIV). Lots of people are led astray by putting man's opinion on the throne of their hearts. A snare is a trap for catching small animals, with the perfect bait to lure the animal into captivity. When you're constantly concerned with the opinions of other people, letting them rule your life, they become a trap for you. The enemy uses your love for people as the perfect bait to lure you into a trap of people pleasing.

Why is it a problem to care so much about what other people think? Well, when we idolize other people's opinions, we're showing fear of man, not fear of God. When we fear the disapproval of others, we're essentially making them gods in our hearts. We often obey what we fear most, so we make decisions based on what other people think instead of what God's Word says.

Maybe you live in constant fear of being exposed as a failure. You wonder what people would think if they found out that you're a fraud. What would people do if they found out that your life isn't actually perfect? What would they do if they found out that you have a past, that your kids aren't well behaved, that your life doesn't actually look like your Instagram feed? What if your social media life were exposed for what it really is? When you constantly fear exposure, it means that you've built an idol of people's opinions. When you spend all your time living in this fear, you don't have time to pursue God's purpose for your life.

In 2 Kings 5, we find a man the Bible calls "a valiant soldier" (2 Kings 5:1 NIV). His name was Naaman, and he served the king of Aram as the commander of his army. According to the Jewish historian Josephus, it was Naaman who drew his bow at random and killed King Ahab (see 1 Kings 22:34).[5] God used Naaman to serve justice, and he became a hero. This simple soldier had become an overnight success, and the people loved him. However, he had a secret: leprosy. The apparent luck that had gained him honor and accolades came crashing down with a dreaded skin disease.

Have you ever known people like this? They were lucky one time, and they brag about it forever. Even if it was luck, they're taking full credit. This is kind of where

Naaman was. Though he had made a career out of one lucky shot, he now had leprosy.

No Pretending

One day, Naaman learned from a slave girl about a prophet who was able to cure diseases. When Naaman told the king of Aram, that king sent him to the king of Israel with a letter. The king of Israel misunderstood and thought that the king of Aram expected him to heal Naaman. The prophet Elisha heard that the king of Israel was upset, and he sent word: "Hey, send Naaman to me."

Elisha's purpose wasn't necessarily to heal the leprosy, but to heal Naaman of the idolatry of public image. When the idol of people's opinions is removed, God can do miraculous things. This is what God was about to do in Naaman.

Proverbs 28:13 says, "Whoever conceals his transgressions will not prosper, but he who confesses and forsakes them will obtain mercy" (ESV). When we're consumed with our image and afraid to be authentic, we aren't following the way of God. Trust me, you don't want to keep your image. Most people can see right through it anyway. We are not as good at concealing it as we think we are.

In my church, we have a saying: "It's okay to not be okay." We don't want people pretending to be something they're not, because the world is fed up with churches behaving this way. We often go to church thinking that everyone there is perfect and, therefore, we don't measure up and don't belong. We forget that the church is full of

people just like us. We're all messed up. We all have issues. We're all broken in different ways.

Authenticity and transparency are key parts of the culture of any great church. We don't have to pretend. We
don't have to be fake. We want people to know the real
God, so we must be real about ourselves, even when it
requires us to be vulnerable.

Craving Honor and Recognition

When we have the idol of F.O.P.O., we crave honor
and recognition. I think this is another reason people leave
church, marriages, and jobs. If they don't feel like they're
treated the way they should be treated, they leave. Have
you ever thought, "I worked late, and nobody even said
thank you! I am never appreciated. No one values me. Nobody sees how great I am!"

The Bible is very clear. Psalm 75:6–7 reveals that pro-
motion doesn't come from the east or west; it comes from
the Lord. If you keep your heart right before the Lord and
He is seated on the throne of your heart, He will know
when to promote you. God takes care of His own. He sees
your actions, whether your boss sees them or not.

When Naaman finally pulled up at Elisha's house, he
got out with all his servants. I'm sure he had an idea in his
mind about what was going to happen. But Elisha didn't
do what was expected when meeting a great military hero;
instead, he sent his servant to meet him. I love how Elisha
downplayed the pomp and circumstance of this meeting!

Elisha sent a message to Naaman: "Go, wash yourself seven times in the Jordan, and your flesh will be restored and you will be cleansed" (2 Kings 5:10 NIV).

Seems simple enough, right? But the idol of people's opinions was so firmly ingrained in Naaman that he didn't even consider it. He took it as a personal rejection that Elisha didn't come out, honor him, and heal him in the way he expected. He said, "I thought that he would surely come out to me and stand and call on the name of the LORD his God, wave his hand over the spot and cure me of my leprosy" (2 Kings 5:11 NIV). Naaman had brought Elisha gifts that amounted to a large sum of money (2 Kings 5:5). Naaman was expecting to buy an instant miracle. He made it about money. He figured, "I'm important: I'm rich, and I'm a hero. I give you money; you give me my miracle!" But Elisha didn't play to that at all, and Naaman was humiliated.

When you fear people's opinions, you will be enraged when you feel rejected. If you live for acceptance, honor, and recognition, you're going to live a life of constant disappointment. We are called to live for the audience of One, to please God and Him alone.

God was working on Naaman. The miracle was waiting right on the other side of his humility and obedience. The same is true for you today. If you fear what people might think of you for worshiping God, then you're idolizing the opinions of others. God wants to sit on the throne of your heart! He wants to exalt Himself through you! Instead, F.O.P.O. may be keeping you from experiencing power, breakthrough, and purpose in your life.

On a mission trip in Nicaragua, we preached at a huge crusade. God was doing miraculous things. People were getting saved by the hundreds. I felt that God wanted to heal people, so I asked people to come forward if they needed healing.

As one particular woman walked up to me, I felt the Lord quicken something in my heart, saying, "I am about to do something miraculous. I am about to heal her." This woman had long hair covering her face, and her head was down. As she stepped forward, I said, "What do you need the Lord to do for you?"

She raised her head up and parted her hair. Her face was covered with a massive tumor. From the top of her head down to her neck, from her nose to her ear, was one solid mass of black, lumpy tumor. Her eye was pressed shut, her nostril was gone, and only part of her mouth was showing. But I knew that it was about to go. As I went to lay hands on her, I felt the Lord say, "Before you do that, she needs Me first."

I said to this beautiful young lady, "I believe that God wants to heal you, but have you ever accepted Christ into your heart?"

She answered, "I don't want that. I just want Him to heal my face."

I asked the interpreter, "Am I saying it wrong?"

He said, "No."

Then I said to the woman, "Ma'am, Jesus wants to be in your heart first before He touches your face."

"I don't want that. Just have Him heal my face."

I took my hand away, saying, "You don't understand. It's not about the outward appearance. God wants your heart. If you give Him your heart, everything else will fall into place."

She wouldn't do it. She walked away from me, refusing to humble herself.

It's easy for us to look at a situation like that and think, "If only she would have listened!" But we do the same thing. We ask God for things, but He is telling us that He wants our hearts. Then we walk away from Him, just like that woman did and like Naaman almost did.

Proverbs 22:4 says, "The reward for humility and fear of the LORD is riches and honor and life" (ESV). When we humble ourselves, we open the door for the miraculous.

Vulnerability

When we put fear of people's opinions upon the throne of our hearts, we become afraid of being vulnerable. This is what keeps a lot of people from experiencing an abundant life in Christ. They refuse to be vulnerable, because they fear what people will think.

As I write this, I'm several weeks into going to a gym. There are some huge bodybuilders there. One of them approached me recently and said, "I want to work out with you. I want to help you."

I said, "Man, you all are on level ten. I'm on level negative four. I'm just a beginner here. I'm just looking to lift a few weights and do some cardio."

He replied, "No, I really feel like I can help you if you'll let me."

Despite my fear, I decided to be vulnerable and trust. I was actually kind of freaked out about being around a bunch of bodybuilders. I mean, they're muscled-up men. I figured that they were probably looking at me and thinking, "Come here, fat boy! Let me poke your belly."

But after some time, I found that they weren't as intimidating as I thought they would be. In fact, they've been some of the most encouraging people ever! They loved that I decided to give it a try.

When people's opinions don't have a hold on you anymore, you gain freedom to try and try again. Just give it a shot. You'll be amazed at the results! God wants to speak to you and give you something better. It's not as intimidating as you think.

Let's look at the aspect of vulnerability in Naaman's story. Naaman's servants said to him, "My father, if the prophet had told you to do some great thing, would you not have done it? How much more, then, when he tells you, 'Wash and be cleansed'!" (2 Kings 5:13 NIV). In other words, "It's so simple. Just try it."

Sometimes we're so caught up in our assumptions about other people's opinions that we miss the possibility that they might simply want to see us get better. They might just want to see us try.

Naaman decided to go down to the river. He "dipped himself in the Jordan seven times, as the man of God had told him, and his flesh was restored" (2 Kings 5:14 NIV). He received fresh skin like a baby's. Naaman allowed himself to be vulnerable for just a moment and respond to the people who loved him. He finally listened and humbled himself, and he was healed.

Craig Groeschel says that "people would rather follow a leader who's always real than one who's always right."[6] When we worry about people's opinions, we forget that people aren't asking us to be right all the time. They would rather we be real! More importantly, no matter what other people want or expect, God wants us to be transparent.

The idol of F.O.P.O. can't just be expelled; it must be replaced. God wants to take that place. In *Counterfeit Gods*, Tim Keller says, "The only way to dispossess the heart of an old affection is by the expulsive power of a new one."[7]

The Bible is clear that "perfect love casts out fear" (1 John 4:18 ESV). When you fear God, you'll fear nothing else. This means that you'll live to please no one but God. You're going to stand before the Lord one day and give an account of your life (Romans 14:12). In the end, His opinion of you is the only one that matters.

REFLECTION

Chapter Three Prompt

Holy Spirit, what are You saying to me?

_____

_____

_____

_____

_____

_____

_____

_____

_____

_____

_____

_____

_____

_____

Holy Spirit, what step(s) do You want me to take?

_____

_____

_____

_____

_____

_____

_____

_____

_____

_____

_____

_____

_____

_____

_____

_____

_____

_____

_____

CHAPTER FOUR

Greater Than F.O.N.H.E.
(Fear of Not Having Enough)

There are some people who claim to love baloney sandwiches, but when you ask them the last time they actually had one, it's usually been a decade or more. When I was growing up as a poor pastor's kid, my family learned to make do with very little. Meals were small, and a baloney sandwich was a rare treat. Most of us have grown past baloney sandwiches. However, there are some people who still eat them. They have no choice, because it's what they're served in jail. (I won't tell you how I know this.) Once they get out, they won't touch baloney sandwiches anymore, because baloney reminds them of being locked up.

When we worship the idol of money—the Fear of Not Having Enough, or F.O.N.H.E. ("phony")—we're putting our hope and faith in phony baloney. As children of God, we should be the way those prisoners are when they're released. We shouldn't buy into phony baloney any longer, because we're free!

Often our biggest source of security, along with our joy and sense of worth, is found in our money and how we spend it. It's only natural for us to feel more relaxed and free when we don't have any debt. When we can't pay a bill, we feel trapped and insecure.

When money is our idol, it becomes our master—the master of our emotions and the master of our choices. Although we can fall into the trap of believing that our security comes from our financial situation, nothing could be further from the truth. It's quite the opposite, actually. Nothing is more insecure than money. Money comes and goes. It's phony baloney.

When we're financially unstable, it's easy for us to start second-guessing God's provision. However, Jesus Himself said, "No one can serve two masters. Either you will hate the one and love the other, or you will be devoted to the one and despise the other. You cannot serve both God and money" (Matthew 6:24 NIV).

God wants to be Lord of all your life, including your money. When we make money our god, we're looking to it as the compass of our lives and our safety net. God is very clear in His Word that He wants us to trust in Him alone. He wants us to acknowledge Him as our provider.

God Can Be Trusted

First Kings 17 says a lot about God's desire to be the source of everything we need. When we arrive on the scene, there's a king who had taken over Israel. King Ahab was an incredibly wicked king. Elijah basically told King Ahab, "Dude, because of your idol worship, there's going to be no rain unless I say so." God then told Elijah to go to a particular valley where He would take care of him through the ravens. The rest of the land wouldn't get rain, but God would provide for Elijah.

Elijah listened, trusting that God would provide as He said He would. And God did supply the food and water Elijah needed so that he could survive the drought. While the rest of the country was paying penance for their idol worship, Elijah got to enjoy the blessings of God in a supernatural way.

I was curious about the place where God sent Elijah. It was called "Kerith Ravine." The Hebrew word *kerîyth* means "to cut or separate."[8] God used a place with this name to trim things from Elijah's life.

I can't help but see a parallel with us today. Sometimes God uses a difficult financial situation or other challenging circumstances in our lives to cut away things that we think we need. This is so we can begin to see that God is a good provider and will keep us safe in His hands, no matter what happens.

When Everything Dries Up

In 1 Kings 17:7, the brook dried up. There are going to be times in your life when things dry up. Whether you follow God or not, there will be resources that you thought you could count on but are no longer there. It may be that you lose a job, you go through a divorce, your loan doesn't get approved, or your house gets repossessed.

For Elijah, the place where God told him to go suddenly wasn't going to sustain him anymore. It was time for him to move on. After the brook dried up, God told Elijah to go to Zarephath. At this point, Elijah must have been pretty concerned about his security. He had lost his food source. But there's good news! God told him that when he made it to Zarephath, there would be a widow who would supply him with food.

This may seem odd, but God can always be trusted. When Elijah made it to the town gate, he saw a woman gathering some sticks. He asked her if she would bring him some water and a piece of bread.

Let me give you some more context. This poor woman had lost her husband, and she had a young son. She was in the middle of this drought, and she was gathering what little she had left to put together one last meal before she and her son would have nothing and would most likely starve to death. Can you imagine? This was the moment when God asked her, through Elijah, for more than she had to give.

This seems like a hard request. I'd have a problem with it! If God told me to ask this widow for food, and I knew the whole context, I would argue with Him: "Why are You asking this of someone who has nothing left to give? She can barely take care of herself and her son. Are You really asking them to step out in faith during a time of famine?" But this is what God does. Remember that Elijah had made his way to a Gentile land. He was among people who didn't know God, and God wanted to reveal Himself to them. Let's read what happened:

> "As surely as the LORD your God lives," she replied, "I don't have any bread—only a handful of flour in a jar and a little olive oil in a jug. I am gathering a few sticks to take home and make a meal for myself and my son, that we may eat it—and die."
>
> Elijah said to her, "Don't be afraid. Go home and do as you have said. But first make a small loaf of bread for me from what you have and bring it to me, and then make something for yourself and your son. For this is what the LORD, the God of Israel, says: 'The jar of flour will not be used up and the jug of oil will not run dry until the day the LORD sends rain on the land.'"
>
> She went away and did as Elijah had told her. So there was food every day for Elijah and for the woman and her family. For the jar of flour was not used up and the jug of oil did not run dry, in keeping with the word of the LORD spoken by Elijah.
>
> **—1 Kings 17:12–16** (NIV)

God called this woman to obedience, and she determined what she was going to do. When we really think about it, what did she have to lose? She was going to die anyway, so she might as well share. Even in the midst of dire circumstances, she was generous and obeyed. Obedience and generosity walk hand in hand.

Signs of F.O.N.H.E.

Many of us bow down before the Fear of Not Having Enough. As I mentioned earlier, it's phony baloney!

God wants to be Lord of our hearts, but time and time again, money captures our attention and our hearts. It promises security, but it can never truly deliver. Let's discuss some ways we can assess if we've made an idol of F.O.N.H.E.

A Delay in Obedience

You know that you've built an altar to F.O.N.H.E. if you don't obey God immediately. God loves to provide, and everything belongs to Him. When He asks you to do something with His blessings and your answer is "no" or "I can't," then you've misused His provisions and made an idol out of them. Sometimes we make bad choices with our money and feel that we can no longer be flexible, but this simply doesn't matter when God speaks.

Psalm 119:60 says, "Without delay I hurry to obey your commands" (GNT). I wish that could be said about me! I want to hurry to do whatever God tells me to do, but there are times when I doubt that He has spoken to me. I may think that God is absent from my life, but how foolish it is to think that God doesn't know my situation. He certainly doesn't need me to explain my situation to Him. He sees me and understands. He knows what He is asking of me.

Legendary coach John Wooden says, "When opportunity knocks, it's too late to get ready."[9] When God is sitting on the throne of our hearts and we're willing to follow His leading immediately, then our answer can always be "yes." When the brook dries up, we don't. We're not left stumbling and fumbling and freaking out. Brooks dry up all the time. God wants us to obey in our lack so that He can lead us to blessing.

In fact, lack can be a teacher. I grew up poor, so I understand that there are powerful lessons you can gain from financial lack that can't come from any other circumstance. You learn things like humility and resourcefulness. You learn how to stretch what you have and that you don't need as much as you thought you did. Tough times teach you to get creative. More than anything else, these times taught me to listen to God.

F.O.N.H.E. is also a teacher—a good teacher of bad habits. We learn how to settle for less than God has for us. We allow things into our hearts that shouldn't be there.

When I was growing up, my family was in ministry and didn't have much at all. There were multiple times when we didn't even have food. Sometimes we would just have an onion, so we would find multiple ways to eat it. To this day, I don't like the taste of onions. It actually makes me sick.

When groceries came to the house, I felt the need to eat the food immediately because I had such a fear that it wouldn't be there the next day. I would gorge myself on anything and everything I could possibly find to eat, and this developed into a bad habit. Even as I grew older, every time there was cereal in the house, I would eat the whole box. My experience with poverty grew in me the Fear of Not Having Enough, which became an idol in my life for years and a stumbling block in my faith.

This may not be how you grew up, but many of us approach money in a way that's not pleasing to God. We remember a time when money dried up in the past, so we hoard it now. We think that the more we save, the smarter we're being. But when it comes time for God to call us to generosity, we don't want to do it. Does this sound familiar? Do you suffer from a fear of not having enough?

If you think that God can't take care of you or you rely on yourself to provide for your needs, you're relying on a foolish idol. F.O.N.H.E. will keep you from experiencing the supernatural provision of God. He won't force you to worship Him, but He stands with His arms open wide and says, "I am a much better provider than you are."

You Would Rather Trust in Unstable Money

One memorable night, I was driving back home by myself after preaching at a youth service. I was thanking the Lord for what had happened and thinking through my week when I got a phone call from my wife. She asked me to pick up diapers for our son on my way home.

After reassuring her that I would handle it, I looked at my fuel gauge and noticed that the gas light had just come on, letting me know that I only had a few gallons left in my truck. Payday was still several days away, so I quickly checked our account. My heart sank when I saw a zero balance. Then I looked in my wallet. All I had left was one ten-dollar bill.

I began to do the math in my head. "Okay, I need money to get back and forth to work. We need to buy groceries for lunches. And my son really needs diapers. So, what am I going to do? Am I going to take the last diaper off of my son and just let him roam around the backyard so nature can take its course? Maybe I can find somebody to ride-share with me for work."

I soon realized how hopeless the situation was. How many diapers could I really buy for ten dollars? I could afford some ramen noodles for lunches, but there's no way I could make this ten-dollar bill take care of all three things. I simply couldn't afford to eat and go back and forth to work and buy my son diapers.

Frustrated, I began to pray: "Okay, Lord, You know that I really need Your help." I began to sense that the Lord was speaking to me in that moment, and He asked me a profound question: "Are you going to trust that ten-dollar bill, or are you going to trust Me?"

I had a tough decision to make. I knew that ten dollars couldn't stretch and do all the things that I needed it to do, but I could feel the Lord asking me to trust Him. I had put my security in that cash, knowing that it wouldn't be enough. In that moment, I decided to make a bold statement of faith. I said, "Okay, Lord, I trust You." Then I rolled down the window and threw the bill to the wind.

The very next day, the Lord began to show up and show us what only He could do. You see, the ten-dollar bill could never have stretched that far, but my God could. He began to provide for us in miraculous ways. Let me just tell you that I never missed a meal, my son always had diapers, and I was able to get back and forth to work because of God's miraculous provision. Over and over, He stepped up and provided for my family in ways that made my jaw drop. I've learned that I can't trust in what I know will not be enough, but I can trust in a God who is Jehovah Jireh. He is always more than enough!

Another sign that you've made F.O.N.H.E. your god is if you would rather trust the instability of money than an ever-present, all-knowing, and all-powerful God. In Mark 10, a rich man came to Jesus and asked, "...what must I do to inherit eternal life?" (Mark 10:17 NIV). The young man told Jesus that he had obeyed all the commandments since he was a kid. Mark 10:21 says, "And Jesus, looking at him, loved him, and said to him, 'You lack one thing: go, sell all that you have and give to the poor, and you will have treasure in heaven; and come, follow me'" (ESV). I love the compassion of our God in this situation. He spoke right into this man's life and told him exactly what he needed to hear. God looks past our own rules and sees what we're missing.

When you build idols to other things, it's not that you have those things, but that those things have you. Jesus looked at this rich young man and told him to get rid of all his stuff. Along with that, He made a promise that he would have so much more treasure in heaven. In that moment, Jesus invited the young man to follow Him. He invited him into relationship. How could he turn that down? But he did! He was actually grieved because of how much he owned, because he didn't want to give it up.

After the young man walked away, Jesus said, "How hard it is for the rich to enter the kingdom of God!" (Mark 10:23 NIV). Why? Because they think that they don't need God. They can write a check for anything they need. God loves to interrupt our comfort to teach us to trust Him, and sometimes He uses material lack to accomplish this purpose.

The widow in 1 Kings made a decision to trust God, but the rich man in Mark 10 walked away. One replaced the idol in her heart. The other said, "No, thanks. I have a fear of not having enough."

Nothing keeps us from obeying God like comfort does. Hebrews 13:5 says, "Keep your life free from love of money, and be content with what you have, for he has said, 'I will never leave you nor forsake you'" (ESV). If you have Jesus, even if you have nothing else, you have more than enough. Be content with what you have. David said, "I have never seen the righteous forsaken or their children begging bread" (Psalm 37:25 NIV). God supernaturally takes care of His own. He is a good Father, not a deadbeat dad. He is not some runaway who leaves His kids to fend for themselves. That's not our God.

An Unhealthy Love of Stuff

People who have made an idol of F.O.N.H.E. will have an unhealthy love of stuff. We often don't acknowledge that loving stuff is deadly to our families in the same way that adultery destroys a marriage. Adultery is a hardcore thing that's a recipe for the end of a marriage. The worship of money is just as damaging. Colossians 3:5 tells us that greed and covetousness are idolatry and we need to put them to death.

I will say it again: love of material things is just as damaging as adultery. Yes, adultery is secretive, and we're afraid to talk about it. We end up going to therapy for it. However, when it comes to money, we put it on display, showing off how much we have. Even so, the Bible says that they're the same. They're equally damaging to our families.

F.O.N.H.E. is a major threat not only to your life, but also to future generations. If you idolize money, your children will spend their lives thinking that money is god. Jesus is clear that you can't serve both. You must make a choice. What do you put your trust in?

One of the top reasons people get divorced is finances. This is why couples don't make it and so many marriages, including Christian ones, end in divorce. When we look at divorce, we think, "Oh, that will never happen to me," but the statistics seem to indicate that there's a chance. If F.O.N.H.E. is on the throne of your heart, you're beaten before you even start.

"My Life Is Only Good If I Have…"

If you've built your life on money, you may think that it's the only thing that makes your life good. This is where the rich young man found himself. He owned too much and was grieved at the thought of giving it up, because he didn't know where real life came from. By the way, the answer was literally staring him right in the face. Talk about a Captain Obvious moment. The source of all life was standing right in front of him, giving him a promise, and he totally missed it.

It's easy for me to bag on this rich young man, but I probably would have done the same thing if I had been in his place. It's hard for the privileged to make that leap, because they don't have desperation like others do.

Sometimes you just need to walk through lack to realize that God is all you need.

In Luke 12:15, Jesus said, "Take care, and be on your guard against all covetousness, for one's life does not consist in the abundance of his possessions" (ESV). If we don't believe that God is able to take care of us, we'll do anything to secure ourselves. Stuff doesn't make a life. Jesus is life!

Jesus said, "I am the living bread that came down from heaven" (John 6:51 NIV). When He taught His disciples to pray, He said, "Give us this day our daily bread" (Matthew 6:11 ESV). I wonder if in this prayer, Jesus was referring to Himself as the bread. F.O.N.H.E. needs to be replaced by the realization that God is so great that nothing can sustain us better than He can. He wants us to feast on Him. He wants us to feast on His Word. But we're too busy eating phony baloney.

Obedient Giving

The only way to dethrone mammon, the god of money, is to replace it with obedient giving. We start by giving to God first. Many Christians will give God whatever is left over. This is not biblical. God wants us to trust Him with our first and our best. Proverbs 3:9 tells us to honor God with our money and our first fruits. God will honor us if we make Him first. This is the same reason we have church on Sunday. We're giving God the first part of our week. God can do more with ninety percent than you can do with one hundred percent, so take a step and honor God by giving to Him.

Give to God not only first, but also gladly! Second Corinthians 9:7 says that "God loves a cheerful giver" (NIV). Don't just give because you have to, but because you want to.

Give to God generously because that's how He gives to us. The most famous scripture of all time says, "For God so loved the world that he gave his one and only Son" (John 3:16 NIV). What did He give? His firstborn Son! Essentially, God tithed His Son. God is a giver, and He gives what is precious to Him.

Many people say that they believe, but they never take a step of faith and honor God with their first and their best. God doesn't need your money, but He asks you to give because it's good for you.

I want to invite you to get rid of the phony baloney. Take God at His word. He is the supernatural provider of all that you need. You serve an amazing God, and He is waiting to show Himself strong on your behalf.

REFLECTION

Chapter Four Prompt

Holy Spirit, what are You saying to me?

_____

_____

_____

_____

_____

_____

_____

_____

_____

_____

_____

_____

_____

_____

Holy Spirit, what step(s) do You want me to take?

_____

_____

_____

_____

_____

_____

_____

_____

_____

_____

_____

_____

_____

_____

_____

_____

_____

_____

_____

CHAPTER FIVE

Greater Than L.I.P.O.
(Labels I Put On)

When I was a kid, I was homeschooled for most of my education. High school was the first time I went to public school in a large city. The school was like one of those schools you see in movies. Drugs and guns were everywhere. Segregation based on race was normal. It was pretty insane. At that point in my life, I had never experienced anything like it, because I had been raised in a Christian bubble. I was like a sheep being thrown into a pack of wolves.

On the first day of school, another student pulled a gun on me. As I'm sure you can imagine, this was pretty shocking for a kid from a Pentecostal church.

From the moment I showed up in suit, tie, khakis, I was labeled as the gay kid. People saw that I was naturally effeminate, so they assumed that I was homosexual. As someone who had been sexually abused by men as a child, I began questioning things. Did they see something in me that even I couldn't see? Would this trauma define me forever?

When you've been a victim of trauma, it's often difficult to distinguish between the lies you've believed and who God has created you to be. Lies become labels, and labels become lifestyles.

This has been a problem since the beginning of time. In Genesis 3, the very first man and woman were tempted by Satan. Satan's plan from the beginning was to make people question God's Word and cause them to self-identify in a way that God never intended. The enemy got Adam and Eve to eat from the tree that God told them not to eat from. They allowed the enemy to deceive them, and as a result, they experienced shame for the first time.

In their shame, Adam and Eve hid from God. God called out to Adam, "Where are you?" (Genesis 3:9 ESV). He was asking why Adam was hiding from Him.

Adam's reply was one of shame. He said, "I was afraid, because I was naked, and I hid myself" (Genesis 3:10 ESV). Adam knew that he had done wrong.

In response, God asked, "Who told you that you were naked?" (Genesis 3:11 ESV). In other words, "Who put that label on you?"

This gets to the heart of what this chapter is about: identity. I call this idol of our identity L.I.P.O., or the Labels I Put On. We all suffer when we allow the world to tell us our place, our identity, and our limitations. The words people speak over us will shape our destiny if we allow them to settle in our hearts. These words can become labels that create a lifestyle. God is asking you, "Who put this label on you? Who told you that you have to live in shame? Who told you that you're naked? How could you allow yourself to believe something so foolish?"

When God created Adam and Eve, He made them without shame (Genesis 2:25). The enemy deceived them by putting this label on them, and they began to see themselves this way, ultimately distancing themselves from God.

When you make an idol of L.I.P.O., it leads to shame and living short of what God has called you to do and be. Only God can tell you who you are and what you're capable of!

The Deceived Deceiver

We can see the idol of L.I.P.O. in the life of Jacob. Jacob had a twin brother named Esau. When they were born, Jacob literally grabbed his brother's leg (Genesis 25:26). As they delivered the twins, they saw that Jacob was being pulled out by his brother. Ultimately, this didn't just become a name for Jacob; it became the essence of who he was—the leg-puller or deceiver. This label ended up taking root in Jacob's heart and defining him.

What's the label on you? Is it actually the truth? Jacob certainly had an identity problem, and these words pushed him into a false destiny. He was not only a deceiver, but was also deceived. However, God saw something more in Jacob. He saw a powerful destiny, a nation, His holy people. God chose Jacob to reveal His nature and will, even while Jacob was being deceived.

Old Labels Are Sticky

In Genesis 32:22–32, Jacob wrestled with God all night. Eventually, God reached down and knocked Jacob's hip out of its socket. This was because Jacob wouldn't give up and wanted to get something out of Him. Jacob was used to scamming, hustling, and taking advantage of people, so he tried to do the same with God. Fortunately for Jacob, God did end up speaking into his destiny. God wanted to rip the label off of his life.

When Jacob was wrestling with God, God spoke right to that label and changed his name from Jacob to Israel. Unfortunately, Jacob's personality didn't change along with his name, and he went on being a deceiver. Old labels are sticky. It took a while for Jacob to walk into his new destiny.

We have no idea how good God is and the destiny He has for us. Many people spend time listening to the enemy, who tells them to keep walking in shame. Like Jacob, we know our destiny, but we easily settle for deception. We allow the labels and definitions others give us to cling to us and change how we see ourselves. We may believe, "I was born this way," but this is why we must be born again. God asks us to step out of our comfort zone and trust Him.

I was five the first time I heard God's voice in my life. He woke me up from a sound sleep and spoke to me very clearly. He said, "I am calling you to preach." I was wide awake, and I looked around for my dad because I was sure that I had heard someone. I didn't start preaching at age six or seven or eight. I was around twenty-five when I started preaching. That's twenty years before I stepped into my calling!

When God exposes the idol of L.I.P.O. in our lives, it can take a while for us to change directions. Even though God has renamed us, it can be difficult for us to believe Him and begin walking in our God-given identity. The slow progress can be discouraging, especially in our microwave culture, which desires instant results.

There's a space between your calling and your destiny, a period of time between God giving you the dream and that dream coming to fruition. This is called sanctification. It's when God changes your character and prepares you to do what He has called you to do. God pulls things out of your heart, pulls the labels off of your life, and draws you to Himself so that you put your hope and trust in Him.

In Genesis 35, Jacob went back to Bethel, where God had revealed his destiny (Genesis 28:10–22) when he was fleeing from Esau. God reminded Jacob that He had removed the label from him and given him a new name. He wanted Jacob to know who he really was. By the way, *Bethel* is another name for "house of God," or the place where the Lord's presence dwells.[10] Sometimes we need to go back to a place where God met us in the past to remember who we really are.

Remove the Idols

At this point, Jacob had his entire family with him, and he told them to get rid of the foreign gods that were with them (Genesis 35:2–4). When you go to meet with God, you also need to rid yourself of the idols you worship. Not only did God want Jacob's household to get rid of the idols, but He also wanted them to be purified. God wants this for you also. He wants you to get your mind right and remove everything that reminds you of your old labels.

Why is it important to remove these things? Because when you're meeting with God, you are entering a holy place! Jacob obeyed God, removing the foreign gods from his household. He buried them and left them behind.

I think this is a prophetic word for us today. There are some things that need to be put to death and buried. Every idol needs to go because God wants to meet us and lead us into our destiny. He wants to transform us into the people we're meant to be.

Genesis 35:5 says, "Then they set out, and the terror of God fell on the towns all around them so that no one pursued them" (NIV). After Jacob's household put away all their idols, God revealed His supernatural provision and protection. God protected His people when they destroyed the things that held them back. The people they came across knew that they shouldn't mess with Jacob or his household. They recognized that God had labeled these people as His own.

The Blessing of Destiny

When you set your heart to bless God with obedience, God will bless you with destiny. Many people expect great things from God but are never willing to take a step of faith and obey Him. The choice is yours!

The story continues in Genesis 35:10–12 (NIV):

God said to him, "Your name is Jacob, but you will no longer be called Jacob; your name will be Israel." So he named him Israel.

And God said to him, "I am God Almighty; be fruitful and increase in number. A nation and a community of nations will come from you, and kings will be among your descendants. The land I gave to Abraham and Isaac I also give to you, and I will give this land to your descendants after you."

The legacy God had given Jacob (now Israel) was bigger than just the one man. God took off the old label of deceiver and gave him a legacy that would affect not only him, but also generations to come. Now that Jacob was walking in obedience, God brought him a generational blessing.

In Bethel, Jacob set up an altar, offered a drink offering to God, and poured out oil for Him (Genesis 35:14). In the Bible, water naturally represents cleansing. Jesus called Himself water (John 4:10, 13–14), and we also see the Word represented by water (Ephesians 5:26). Oil represents the Holy Spirit (Matthew 25:1–13). Both the Word and the Holy Spirit, water and oil, help you to understand what it's like to walk in the fullness of what God has called you to do and be. Once you rid yourself of L.I.P.O., you can walk into this new and abundant life!

A New Creation

When we carry around the labels of our old life, they define us and direct the choices we make. These labels become idols when they call the shots in our lives, but God wants to be the one to give us our identity, purpose, and direction.

There's someone greater than your pain and regrets, and it's time to start listening to and obeying Him. Like Jacob, we are being called to put God on the thrones of our hearts. God is reminding us of who we are. Will you let God define you? You must decide, because L.I.P.O. cannot coexist with the identity God has given you.

Second Corinthians 5:17 calls us new creations. We need to bury the old things, the foreign gods we have collected. In Jeremiah 2:13, God said, "My people have committed two sins: They have forsaken me, the spring of living water, and have dug their own cisterns, broken cisterns that cannot hold water" (NIV). Our identities apart from Christ cannot sustain us, yet we continue to return to those labels. We forget who we are and who God is. We choose to believe the lie of our old labels over the calling of God, but these labels simply cannot satisfy us. The source of life is holding His hand out to us. Instead of settling for L.I.P.O., we should choose living water!

Romans 4:17 calls God the one "who gives life to the dead and calls into being things that were not" (NIV). You may not see it or feel it, but God is calling things out of you that you don't even know are there. He sees the things that are buried within you and rips off the label on the outside to reveal them. He breathes on us and brings us back to life.

You may not feel like a new creation in Christ. You may not think that you are the person God's Word says you are. But following after God isn't a feeling; it's a choice. Choices lead, and feelings follow.

In 2 Thessalonians 1:11, Paul said that he was praying that God would make the church worthy of His calling. When you read this verse, notice that the calling is *His*. You may think that the calling is yours, but ultimately, it's God's!

Paul also said that the gifts and calling of God are irrevocable (Romans 11:29). *Irrevocable* would be better translated as "without regrets."[11] What would it be like to live a life without regrets? This is a life that lives on purpose for God. It's a life that is led from one obedient step to the next.

The Authority of the Word

Dethroning the idol of L.I.P.O. only happens when you replace it with the authority of God's Word. We can't just remove our labels. We must replace them with something greater.

In John 17, Jesus was praying for His disciples. He prayed, "Sanctify them by the truth; your word is truth" (John 17:17 NIV). God's truth will sanctify you!

Idols aren't replaced by good intentions. They're replaced by a God who is greater than they are. Cleaning you up is God's job, and He is very good at it. God said, "I will sprinkle clean water on you, and you will be clean; I will cleanse you from all your impurities and from all your idols" (Ezekiel 36:25 NIV). God removes the labels from your life. He cleans them right off.

When you leave it up to God, He changes you. When I began to allow the Lord to define me, He sanctified my heart. He gave me a supernatural hunger for His Word, and I began to devour it. I couldn't let even a day pass without reading it. When you're trying to destroy L.I.P.O., start by reading God's Word.

In sixth grade, my science teacher was named Miss Krasinski. She was a Russian lady who spoke very little English, and what English she did speak was spoken with a thick Russian accent. She was hardcore and yelled quite a bit. The only other place I'd been where people yelled randomly was at church on Sunday mornings. This lady intimidated me.

If I knew the answer to one of her questions, I would raise my hand. On my first day, I got the answer wrong, and she said, "That was stupid." I'd never been called stupid, and even though she was referring to my answer, I took it personally.

I began to act out in her class, and she ended up calling a parent–teacher conference. At the conference, Miss Krasinski said to my parents, "He's far less intelligent than the rest of the class and very far behind."

When I heard that comment, I heard again that I was stupid, and I began to cry. My parents asked me what was happening in the class, so I told them, "She hates me!" From that moment, I began to believe that I was stupid. I carried that label with me for a long time, and I actually lived it out. I had a hard time wrapping my mind around things that other people understood. I'm actually a three-time college dropout because I carried that label of "stupid." I let it define me and make me lazy. I didn't want to do the work, because I figured that I wasn't smart enough to do it.

"You know, you're really smart. You are pretty good at this." Something was broken off of me when a pastor said those words to me. All it took was one moment of encouragement from someone I respected and it was as if he had removed a label I'd been wearing for twenty years.

What lies have you chosen to believe? What has defined you? What has kept you from becoming who God has called you to be?

It's time to bury those things, once and for all. You can absolutely do this! Jesus' blood speaks a better word! There are many people who have gone before you, many whose labels were removed. God changed Abram's name to Abraham (Genesis 17:5) and Sarai's name to Sarah (Genesis 17:15). God changed Simon to Peter (John 1:42), the rock He would build His church on (Matthew 16:18)—or Rocky, as I like to call him.

David was a shepherd boy, and God chose him to defeat the giant Philistine named Goliath and eventually become king. When God sent the prophet Samuel to anoint the next king of Israel, even Samuel was deceived by outward labels (1 Samuel 16:1–13). He was looking for a handsome guy with great height and broad shoulders. But there's hope for the ugly ones like me because God doesn't look at the outward appearance. He looks at the heart.

Who told you that you're naked? Who told you that you're gay? Who told you that you're stupid? Who told you that you're going to be single your whole life? Who gets to define you?

God will use His Word to wash off the labels. His Word reverses the curse. He calls you "beloved" (Song of

Songs 6:3 NIV) and "highly favored" (Luke 1:28 NIV). He calls you "the head and not the tail" (Deuteronomy 28:13 ESV). He says that you're the righteousness of God in Christ (2 Corinthians 5:21). He says, "I choose you." The question is: do you choose Him, or do you choose the label?

REFLECTION

Chapter Five Prompt

Holy Spirit, what are You saying to me?

_____

_____

_____

_____

_____

_____

_____

_____

_____

_____

_____

_____

_____

_____

Holy Spirit, what step(s) do You want me to take?

_____

_____

_____

_____

_____

_____

_____

_____

_____

_____

_____

_____

_____

_____

_____

_____

_____

_____

_____

_____

CHAPTER SIX

Greater Than W.I.T.I.C.H.
(What I Think I Can Handle)

When I was a teenager, I was invited to a fair on the Fourth of July. If you have never been to Texas in July, you may not understand, but let me tell you that the heat is unbearable. I went on one of those rides that spins around so fast that you get stuck to the walls. This was never a good idea, especially since I'm not into carnival rides. Some people love those sorts of things, but I'm not one of them. I'm a control freak, and this ride was made for people who love being out of control. I like things to be manageable, and I don't like surprises. I like knowing what to expect.

Against my better judgment, I agreed to go on this ride. It started spinning around and around and around—and it wouldn't stop! It was stuck! People were screaming around me, and I remember thinking, "Where are You, God? This is nuts!" They couldn't shut the ride off for what seemed like forever. What should have been a two-minute ride turned into twenty minutes of hell. I'm sure you can imagine that it got pretty bad. What started off as happiness turned into chaos and screaming and chain-reaction vomiting.

They ended up having to cut the power to the ride. Everything went dark, but it took a while for the ride to slow down. People were dropping to the floor, which was covered in hot puke. It was utterly disgusting. Desperate, I belly crawled my way to the door in an effort to escape the heat and the horrible stench.

I think this nightmarish experience paints a picture of what can happen in life. Sometimes life spins out of control. You're desperate to get out of the crazy, but all you can do is hang on to something and try to make some sense of what is happening.

There are times in our lives when God uses chaos to lead us back to Him. We may be lulled into a false sense of control as we go through our daily routines. It takes everything falling apart or spinning wildly out of control to show us that only God remains the same. The next idol we're going to address is What I Think I Can Handle, or W.I.T.I.C.H.

In 2020, the year of the coronavirus pandemic, I think that we all felt something like this. Life quickly changed in ways we'd never experienced before. We all held on for dear life, just trying to catch our breath. We didn't really understand what was happening, and we had no idea what the future would hold. Then, when it came to election season, it seemed like vomit was everywhere. We were disoriented, scared, and desperate to control anything we could.

As crazy as life is, our desire to control things can become an idol. We think that if we have control and can keep a good handle on our lives, everything will be okay. But I believe that God can actually use chaos to change the world. He is asking us to release control and trust Him in the chaos.

Grasping for Control

Old Testament judges were deliverers and warriors. God raised up these judges to lead His people out of idolatry and into victory. However, time and time again, after every victory, the people of Israel would make their way right back into idolatry.

This is what happened in Judges 6. God's people kept returning to their idols, looking for things they could put their hope in when everything seemed to be spiraling out of control. At this point, God let them be bullied by the Midianites yet again.

In Judges 6, God raised up a young man named Gideon. Before God rescued His people, they were stuck hiding in caves. They couldn't feed their families or their flocks. Every time they would farm, the Midianites would come and destroy everything or seize it from them.

The people of Israel were at a low point, and they cried out to the Lord for help. Let's read the story:

> *When the people of Israel cried out to the Lord on account of the Midianites, the Lord sent a prophet to the people of Israel. And he said to them, "Thus says the Lord, the God of*

> *Israel: I led you up from Egypt and brought you out of the house of slavery. And I delivered you from the hand of the Egyptians and from the hand of all who oppressed you, and drove them out before you and gave you their land. And I said to you, 'I am the LORD your God; you shall not fear the gods of the Amorites in whose land you dwell.' But you have not obeyed my voice."*
>
> **—Judges 6:7–10** *(ESV)*

The people of Israel weren't facing punishment without cause. They created this chaos.

There are a lot of well-meaning Christians who still miss what God is trying to tell them. God is calling them to turn away from the way they're living. They bow down to the idols of the culture and do what everyone else is doing. God is calling them to come out and be different. He wants them to let go of the world's ways of trying to control things.

Like the people of Israel, we're prone to grasp for control in the midst of chaos. This is the idol of What I Think I Can Handle. Essentially, we make ourselves into gods because we think that it's up to us to handle everything that happens in our lives. Jonah 2:8 says, "Those who cling to worthless idols turn away from God's love for them" (NIV). Control is a worthless idol!

Nothing is going to be more stable than our God. Nothing else brings peace during times of chaos like He does. How can you turn away from this amazing love and worship something that's worthless? The idol of W.I.T.I.C.H. runs in direct contradiction to the leading of the Holy Spirit.

Following God and grasping for control cannot go hand in hand, whether you're working in a business, at home, or serving in ministry. My church doesn't belong to me. It's the Lord's church, and He is going to do what He wants to do. I don't get much of a say in it. The more I try to take control, the more I hear Him asking me to give it up. If you're walking in God's will, you don't own anything. It all belongs to Him—your business, your family, your ministry. It's all His, and you're just a steward of it.

I'm sure that I'm not the only one who feels like life makes sense when I get a fresh haircut and my lawn is perfectly manicured. If my flower beds look good, I feel just fine. It gives me a sense of accomplishment and pride. Life seems like it has some meaning to it. But the sense of purpose and fulfillment we get from these trivial things is just on the surface. The feeling that we're in control is an illusion. It's not real, and it won't last.

Identifying W.I.T.I.C.H.

In Judges 6, we find Gideon hiding from the Midianites, threshing wheat in a wine press. He knew that there was chaos outside the walls of the winepress, but he was comfortable inside of it. It was what he thought he could handle and the place where he felt in control.

We like to pretend that we have control. We grasp for it, but in vain, because God is actually the one in control. We look in all the wrong places and end up building an altar to W.I.T.I.C.H. We want to do things our way. When we do this, we ignore what God may be trying to lead us to do and become. Here are some ways to identify when we've made an idol of W.I.T.I.C.H.

A God I Can Manage

The first clue that we're building an altar to the god of control is if we want a God we can manage. We want the God who heals, provides, helps, and delivers when we ask Him to, but we don't want the God who asks us to step out in faith. We don't want the God who leads us to share our testimony. We want a God who listens to us and does what we ask Him to do. We want a God who serves us and asks nothing of us. Who's really God when this is the God we're looking for? Who's the one giving orders here?

A. W. Tozer said, "Grace will save a man but it will not save him and his idol."[12] He wants to save you, not your view of who He is. You need to come to Him on His terms.

In Matthew 26:39, Jesus cried out to His Father. He prayed, "My Father! If it is possible, let this cup of suffering be taken away from me. Yet I want your will to be done, not mine" (NLT). What a great example of what to do when life sucks! When chaos reigns and things don't go the way we think they should go, we find our example in Jesus Himself. Jesus gave God control and trusted Him. He understood that God isn't someone we can manage. God doesn't want to be anybody's copilot.

God Can't Use Me

Another sign that you're worshiping W.I.T.I.C.H. is if you think that God uses people to do great things, but He can't use you. We see this in multiple people throughout the Bible. In Exodus 4:10–17, Moses tried to convince God that he wasn't the right man to lead the Israelites out of Egypt. He said, "God, You have the wrong guy. Send my brother. He's a much better speaker than I am. He's available. He's only working part-time. He's got a much better beard. He's got a better face for television than I have."

Elijah, too, had this problem. In 1 Kings 19:4, he said, "God, I'm done. Just take my life from me. It's over." Jonah also refused God's calling. He said, "No, thanks. I believe that You are an amazing God. You do wonderful things, but not me, buddy!"

Many of us have had the same issue. We say, "Lord, I believe in You, but please use somebody else. I'd rather have control of my life. I don't want a God I have to trust in. I just want a God who does what I ask." If you think this way, you're worshiping a false god, my friend. As Tim Keller says, "If your god never disagrees with you, you might just be worshiping an idealized version of yourself."[13]

Often what makes us the most afraid exposes what we haven't really given to God. When things seem out of control, it can tell us a story. It can reveal parts of our hearts that we've kept for ourselves.

"Before I Move…"

When control is our god, everything has to make sense to us before we move. We ask God to prove Himself to us before we take the next step.

Not a lot of people in history got to talk to the Lord face to face, but when Gideon got his chance, he said, "All right, if you really are from God, then I'm going to bring you a meal." The Lord reached down and consumed the entire meal in fire (Judges 6:17–21).

Have you ever been there? You might have felt God showing you something. In fact, it was very clear what He was asking of you, but instead of obeying Him immediately, you said, "I'm going to need just a little bit more, Jesus."

Gideon did this. He kept asking God for more proof. He took a piece of lamb skin, laid it out, and asked God to make the fleece completely wet, but the ground around it completely dry (Judges 6:36–38). Well, God did it. Then Gideon asked Him to do the opposite (Judges 6:39–40). He said, "I'm going to set this out one more night, God. Make the ground around it wet and the fleece dry. Then I'll know that what You are saying is true."

God was so patient with Gideon, and He is patient with us, too. We always want clarity and reassurance, don't we? We don't want to step out in faith when we don't see how all of the pieces fit together. We think that's just for spiritual people who live on the edge.

The reality is that we're not always going to understand what God is doing. Even the apostle Paul said, "For now we see in a mirror dimly" (1 Corinthians 13:12 ESV). We can't make things out perfectly, and God doesn't always explain Himself. Still, He is often very patient with us. He doesn't have to explain Himself, but sometimes He will give us confirmation of His will and promises.

Isaiah 55:9 says, "As the heavens are higher than the earth, so are my ways higher than your ways and my thoughts than your thoughts" (NIV). Your natural mind isn't going to understand God's ways. Once you recognize this, you'll see that the desire for control runs in contradiction to the Holy Spirit's leading.

First Corinthians 2:14 says, "The natural person does not accept the things of the Spirit of God" (ESV). It's not always going to make sense. You won't have perfect clarity. You won't have one-hundred-percent certainty like Gideon did, but everything is going to work out.

There are many Christians who miss this truth about what it means to give our hearts and lives to God and follow Christ. We're told that we can know God and have an intimate relationship with Jesus, but no one ever tells us that this comes from a daily yielding to the power of the Holy Spirit. So many people are afraid of the Holy Spirit because they're afraid that they'll lose control. Yes, you will lose control, and that's precisely what needs to happen.

Time to Explode

When God called Gideon, he was in a place where he was just getting by. But God didn't design us to get by; He designed us to explode. There's a big difference between existing and exploding. We tend to settle for W.I.T.I.C.H., our own sense of normalcy, when God wants to give us so much more.

The angel called Gideon out and said that he was a "mighty man of valor" (Judges 6:12 ESV). Gideon argued with God (Judges 6:15). He said, "No, I'm not a mighty man. I'm the least of my brothers. You're talking to someone from the smallest clan. You have the wrong number. Go talk to someone who's big and strong. I'm a nobody."

Gideon wasn't easy to convince. Not only that, but he also accused God of being absent (Judges 6:13). He wondered where God had been in the midst of all the chaos his people were experiencing. But God said to him, "I will be with you, and you shall strike the Midianites as one man" (Judges 6:16 ESV). It was God's presence and power that enabled Gideon to leave the place he thought he could handle and explode into the destiny God had for him.

It's the same for us. We give up control through the daily leading of the Holy Spirit. I can't say it more plainly than that. It takes being led by the Spirit for us to give up control.

This has been my most difficult battle as a pastor. As my church continues to grow, I have to move past things I can't control. I have to learn to trust people on my staff to handle things I would normally do. When we were a small church, I could take time to sit with people and answer their questions. As things began to grow, I could no longer sit down with every person who came to my office with questions. I just didn't have the time, and it didn't make sense anymore for me to do it.

I had to start asking myself, "Am I the only one who can answer this question? Because if someone else can respond to this, I should let that person go first." This was a hard adjustment for me, but I had to learn to let go. As I started releasing control, I began to see growth in myself, our staff, and our church.

It was hard to let go when my kids were learning how to drive. Whenever I felt that they weren't going to stop in time, I would press on the imaginary brake and grab the door handle for added security—but of course, it didn't work. Then I had to release them to drive the streets on their own. I have my bases covered, though, because I got full-coverage insurance!

One day, my kids will move out of the house, and my wife and I will become empty nesters. In every season of life, there's a chance either to hold on tightly to what we think we can handle or to put everything in God's hands, knowing that He can do a better job with it. God can do a much better job of leading my church. He can do a better job of raising my children.

I don't know about you, but I don't want to be one of those people who refuse to let go of control and choose to worship a god of their own making. I don't want to worship some false view of God. I want to worship the God who does what He wants and chooses to include me. I want to be carried by the Holy Spirit. That isn't easy, especially for a big guy like me!

Romans 8:14 says, "For all who are led by the Spirit of God are sons of God" (ESV). This is how you know the difference between someone who is the real deal and someone who bows down to some other version of God. Real control is letting go of control and giving it to the God who has ultimate control.

God said, "In the last days, ... I will pour out my Spirit on all people" (Acts 2:17 NIV). This is beautiful, but I think that we ignore it because we believe that the Holy Spirit is reserved for super-spiritual people. This is simply not the case. God's Spirit is available to those who ask. The last days began when God sent His Holy Spirit, so we are absolutely in the last days. The Spirit of God is still available, and He is asking us to yield to Him. Our world is in chaos. Will you allow God to be Lord of your life?

In Judges 7:1–8, God took Gideon's army and narrowed it down to just three hundred men. At that point, it seemed impossible to defeat their enemies, but God promised to grant victory although they were outnumbered. He wanted to prove to the people of Israel that He was in control.

God wasn't looking for a bunch of people who could fight. He was looking for a bunch of people who were going to make some noise and shed some light. And that's what they did. They screamed, hollered, and blew trumpets, and God brought the victory. He brought victory with just three hundred people who were faithful to Him. It's time to let go of control and let the Holy Spirit lead us from just existing to exploding!

REFLECTION

Chapter Six Prompt

Holy Spirit, what are You saying to me?

_____

_____

_____

_____

_____

_____

_____

_____

_____

_____

_____

_____

_____

Holy Spirit, what step(s) do You want me to take?

_____

_____

_____

_____

_____

_____

_____

_____

_____

_____

_____

_____

_____

_____

_____

_____

_____

_____

_____

_____

CHAPTER SEVEN

Greater Than F.O.T.A.S.
(Fear of Taking a Step)

Linus in *Charlie Brown* had a blanket.[14] It was pretty nasty, and his friends criticized him for it. It was his literal security blanket, something he used to soothe himself and keep himself calm. We all probably had something like that as children. There's a point in life when we're supposed to outgrow those security items. Unfortunately, most people just trade the security blanket in for something else. We constantly look for things that will give us security.

When the Lord began to move in my heart to uproot my family from Fort Worth and move to Longview, Texas, to pastor a church there, I knew that it would take some kind of miracle for this to happen. First of all, we didn't know anyone in Longview. We had zero relationships there. Second, to take over this church would mean a significant pay cut for me. Third, my wife and I would be leaving behind a lot of family and friends. I knew that it would be a particularly difficult adjustment for my children to leave their school, friends, and family.

With all of these things and more to consider, it was a big deal for me to step out in faith and trust the Lord that what I was hearing was actually His voice. I began to pray, "Okay, Lord, I feel like this is where You are asking me to go, so I'm going to start stepping out in faith." And as we started to take those steps, the Lord began doing some incredible things.

One of the biggest hurdles we needed to get over involved my wife's job. She was employed as a teacher and couldn't break her contract in the middle of the year, so we knew that we needed a major breakthrough for us to be able even to consider such a move.

Once we decided to pursue this move, my wife talked to her employer and let them know what was happening. The principal of the school said, "The only way we can replace you midway through the school year is if someone with your same qualifications comes to replace you." This would be a rare thing, as my wife was highly qualified to teach special-needs children. That day, a former teacher who had my wife's exact qualifications showed up asking if there were any job openings. She interviewed the same day, and they offered her the job, allowing my wife to get out of her teaching contract.

One of the other major obstacles involved our house. We knew that we'd have to sell it, and at that time, the housing market in the area was cold. There were many houses that had been sitting on the market for months. Nevertheless, we took a step of faith and listed our home. Nine days later, we had a potential buyer. This guy needed to buy three houses before the year was over, because his father had passed away and left him a bunch of money. If he didn't invest the money in real estate fast, he would have to pay a large amount in taxes on the gift. He asked if he could buy our house and told us that we could continue to live in it as long as we needed. The wild thing was that it was a cash offer for *double* what we had originally paid for our house! Here was God, once again showing up in an undeniable way.

Looking back, I'm still in awe of how God worked in our situation—not only getting my wife out of a contract and finding someone to fill her place, but also arranging for us to sell our house in a down market for double what we had paid only two years prior. It was and still is a powerful example of how, as we step forward in faith, God moves to do what only He can do on our behalf.

We want to believe that God gives us constant safety. We may think, "As long as I worship God and go to church on Sunday, nothing bad can happen to me, right? God won't ever ask me to step out of my comfort zone. I've paid my tithes. He won't bring discomfort into my life." This mindset points to our tendency to make an idol out of security. It's a false view of who God is and what it takes to worship Him. First John 5:21 says, "Little children, guard yourselves from idols" (NASB).

God is our true peace and security, but there are many times when He calls us to step out into the great unknown. When He does this, it's scary and doesn't make sense to us. As long as we hold on to our false beliefs, we won't ever take a step of faith.

Maybe you're asking God, "When will You step in?" and He is saying to you, "When will you step out?" I like to call the idol of security the Fear of Taking a Step, or F.O.T.A.S.

The Culture of Athens

When Paul was waiting for Silas and Timothy in Athens, "he was greatly distressed to see that the city was full of idols" (Acts 17:16 NIV). The thing that distressed Paul wasn't that the Greeks had idols but that the Jews and God-fearing Greeks in Athens participated in worshiping them! They knew better, but they hadn't influenced the culture. Instead of infiltrating the culture, they were letting the culture infiltrate them.

Some Epicurean and Stoic philosophers debated with Paul. They asked, "What is this babbler trying to say?" (Acts 17:18 NIV). Others thought that Paul was trying to get people to worship foreign gods because he was preaching about Jesus. They took him to a meeting at the Areopagus, a place where philosophers would gather to discuss various ideas. There they asked Paul to explain the new ideas he was presenting.

Luke inserted his own parenthetical statement here: "All the Athenians and the foreigners who lived there spent their time doing nothing but talking about and listening to the latest ideas" (Acts 17:21 NIV). He was basically saying that these people were nothing but talk. They listened to the latest ideas, but that's all they did. They had the idol of F.O.T.A.S. and did nothing with the ideas they heard.

Paul stood up and began telling them about the one true God. He said, "People of Athens! I see that in every way you are very religious. For as I walked around and looked carefully at your objects of worship, I even found an altar with this inscription: TO AN UNKNOWN GOD" (Acts 17:22–23 NIV).

We can never really understand who God is when we are constantly trying to control the next step. God's ways can sometimes be a mystery to us, so we search out the things that are easier for us to understand. We choose to put our faith and hope in those things instead of in the one true God.

Paul went on to say: "So you are ignorant of the very thing you worship—and this is what I am going to proclaim to you. The God who made the world and everything in it is the Lord of heaven and earth and does not live in temples built by human hands. He is not served by human hands, as if he needed anything. Rather, he himself gives everyone life and breath and everything else" (Acts 17:23–25 NIV). God doesn't need people to serve Him. He doesn't need anything from us. What God really wants is our trust!

Paul continued: "From one man he made all the nations, that they should inhabit the whole earth; and he marked out their appointed times in history and the boundaries of their lands. God did this so that they would seek him and perhaps reach out for him and find him, though he is not far from any one of us" (Acts 17:26–27 NIV).

I love this about our God! He wants us to reach out to Him. He wants us to know Him. All it takes is a step of faith. He is such a gentleman that He just holds out His hand and asks us to come to Him. How does He do this? By placing us in the perfect place at the perfect time to hear from Him. He calls us to stop our worship of fallible things and to place Him on the throne of our hearts.

Unfortunately, we would rather know the god of F.O.T.A.S. We desire security in what we know, in what is familiar and comfortable to us. It's hard to trust something that we're not sure of yet. How do we know if we're basing our lives on the Fear of Taking a Step? I think that we can gain some insight by examining Athenian culture, especially when it came to the Jews and Greeks who worshiped God. Although this time is far removed from us, let's look at how these aspects of Athenian culture are still relevant today.

They Loved to Talk

The Athenians loved to theorize and talk. It might have been about spiritual things, but not necessarily about knowing God. They listened to and debated different ideas, but they never did anything else with those ideas.

Pastors today are notorious for this. We talk and talk and talk. We talk about the things God is going to do and how we believe He will pour out His Spirit. We may talk about a "someday" or a "revival" coming in the future, but we rarely do more than talk.

God's greatest hope is that we will trust and obey Him because we love Him. Instead, we busy ourselves with looking at "someday" and avoid taking a step today. *Someday*, when my money gets right, I'll be generous. *Someday* I'll step out and serve someone else. *Someday*

I'll join a church. *Someday* I'll worship with my hands raised. *Someday* I'll take a step of faith. But not today.

We're afraid to take a step into the unknown, so we stay in our talk of someday and focus on the things we can see, understand, and control. This approach to life will keep us from knowing the destiny God has for each of us.

They Did Nothing with Reason

The people in Athens loved to listen to reason, but they didn't do anything with it. You can deliver clever arguments, make perfect points, or hear a powerful sermon, but if you don't do anything with it come Monday, how good was it really? Does what you hear and say on Sunday really affect your Monday? If the answer is "no," then the idol of F.O.T.A.S. may have a stronghold in your heart.

This is a problem for Christians living in American culture. We love the God of the Bible; we just don't love the God who calls us to *live* the Bible. We love Jesus as long as He doesn't require anything of us. We love God as long as He doesn't call us to be something other than what we want to be. God calls us to trust and obey Him. These sound like simple words, but they're not easy to put into practice.

They Were Paralyzed

A telltale sign of the idol of F.O.T.A.S. in people's lives is that they appear religious but are paralyzed by fear. They say all the right things and even seem to do the right things, but they don't make any progress. The Bible calls this "faith without works" (James 2:26 NASB).

> *What good is it, my brothers and sisters, if someone claims to have faith but has no deeds? Can such faith save them? Suppose a brother or a sister is without clothes and daily food. If one of you says to them, "Go in peace; keep warm and well fed," but does nothing about their physical needs, what good is it? In the same way, faith by itself, if it is not accompanied by action, is dead.*
>
> *But someone will say, "You have faith; I have deeds."*
>
> *Show me your faith without deeds, and I will show you my faith by my deeds.*
>
> **—James 2:14–18** (NIV)

Isn't it obvious that God talk without God acts is outrageous nonsense? Like The Message Bible says, "Faith and works, works and faith, fit together hand in glove" (James 2:18 MSG). James also said that if you're not willing to take care of orphans and widows, your faith is worthless (James 1:27).

God doesn't save you based on how good you are. That's not what I'm saying. However, He did save you to do something with that saving faith. There are people around you who need you, and God wants you to step up. He wants you to take a step of faith. It's uncomfortable, but God wants you to get comfortable with being uncomfortable.

What are you doing with your salvation? What are you doing with your faith? God doesn't want you merely to say a prayer and get your fire insurance or your get-out-of-jail-free card. He wants you to live the rest of your life for His glory, making a difference with all your days.

Personally, this is what I ultimately hope for in my life. I want God to use me, in whatever time I have left, to encourage and strengthen as many people as possible and point them to the unknown God. I want to do more than talk. I want to walk the walk. My answer to God needs to be: "Yes, I trust You."

God challenges us to go beyond what we think we can do. He calls us to step into the supernatural and become something more than what we're comfortable with.

God never calls us to safety or comfort. That will come when we reach heaven, but in the meantime, we've got a lot of living to do. Our job is to get as many people to heaven with us as possible. That can't happen if the church is paralyzed because we've built an altar to F.O.T.A.S.

What would happen if you were to use your faith and actually take a step? What if you succeed? You just may find God in the unknown place beyond your comfort.

You might tell me, "Well, pastor, I believe that God can do anything with *you*, but not with me." This is where we find a lot of Christians today. They believe in the God of the Bible until it comes time to do something about it.

Hebrews 11 talks about a hall of fame filled with the great faith pioneers who have gone before us; it mentions several of these heroes by name. Abraham believed, but he did more than believe; he got up and moved (Genesis 12). Moses didn't just believe. He got up and led two million people out of slavery (Exodus 3–14). Noah didn't just believe; he started building a boat when rain was a foreign concept (Genesis 6–7).

Another great example of this is David (1 Samuel 17). David didn't just believe. He grabbed a rock. He didn't focus on Goliath's size. Instead, he told Goliath how God was greater than anything or anyone who opposed Him.

A friend of mine visited Israel and went down to the Valley of Elah, where David slew Goliath. He grabbed a rock from the brook that runs from the middle of the valley and brought it back to me. That rock is a reminder to me of how small things can be used powerfully in the hands of a great God. Giants fall when God's people take steps of faith. If we're too busy building an altar to the Fear of Taking a Step to put our faith into practice, we won't get to see God move. He wants to replace this idol with something greater than our fears.

Take a Step

Instead of worshiping F.O.T.A.S., let's dethrone it! Second Corinthians 5:7 tells us that "we walk by faith" (ESV). Faith does more than talk; it spurs us to action. Faith is walking.

We've become too comfortable with hearing a sermon. We need to walk it out. We're not just going to remove F.O.T.A.S. We're going to replace it with action because faith always takes a step. It doesn't have to be a secure step. It can be a shaky step. It can be a tiny shuffling of the feet, but even that's movement toward the Lord. Are you willing to try? Are you willing to respond to His call?

In Matthew 14:22, Jesus told His disciples to go across the lake. Just before dawn, when it was the darkest, Jesus went out to meet them, walking on the lake. When His disciples saw Him, they were terrified. They thought that He was a ghost. They were paralyzed with fear because they saw God doing something supernatural.

Jesus immediately told them, "Take courage!" (Matthew 14:27 NIV). The Greek word used here means to "make bold."[15] I believe that God is calling His people to be emboldened today.

One of the disciples, Peter, got a bright idea. He thought, "Wait a sec. If Jesus can do this, maybe I can." He called out to Jesus, "Lord, if it's you, ... tell me to come to you on the water" (Matthew 14:28 NIV). "Tell me" is translated in another version as "command me" (Matthew 14:28 ESV). Peter didn't just want to walk to Jesus; he wanted to walk at the word of Jesus. He realized that if Jesus gave him the word, he could do things far beyond his comfort zone, even things that the world thought were crazy or impossible.

When you step into the great unknown, you'll find that Jesus meets you there. Peter might have taken only a few steps, but that's more than anyone else in the boat did. No one else had the courage to step out of the boat and try to walk on water. I wonder what I would have done. Would I have had the faith to put away the idol of F.O.T.A.S. and step into the impossible?

After taking a few steps, Peter looked at the wind and the waves, and then he started sinking. This was the human response to the situation. Jesus reached down and said, "You of little faith" (Matthew 14:31 NIV). I used to read that as an insult. But Jesus made it clear that it only takes a little bit of faith to move mountains (Matthew 17:20), so it might actually have been a compliment!

Is it scary to take a step of faith? Yes. Is it worth it? Absolutely! My friend, I want to encourage you to stop building an altar to F.O.T.A.S. Stop worshiping security and familiarity. God is calling you into the great unknown, and this is where you'll meet Him in a whole new way. This is where you'll become who God has always meant for you to be.

Your first step might be to repent from a particular sin. It might be to lift your hands during worship next time you're at church. Maybe your next step will be to talk with God if you haven't made that part of your daily life. If you've never set foot in a church, maybe that's your next step. Or maybe it's time for you to go back to church if you haven't been in a while. Whatever it is for you, put your faith to work and take the first step!

REFLECTION

Chapter Seven Prompt

Holy Spirit, what are You saying to me?

_____

_____

_____

_____

_____

_____

_____

_____

_____

_____

_____

_____

_____

Holy Spirit, what step(s) do You want me to take?

_____

_____

_____

_____

_____

_____

_____

_____

_____

_____

_____

_____

_____

_____

_____

_____

_____

_____

_____

_____

_____

CONCLUSION

Know Him

An older couple was in the car, driving to church, when the wife said, "Do you remember when we used to be so close that I would snuggle up to you and lean my head on your shoulder? Now I'm way over here on my side. What happened to us?"

To this, the husband replied, "You moved."

Whenever we spot a problem or issue in our relationship with God, we can be certain that we're the ones who moved. Or perhaps we were never all that close to God in the first place and never entered into a real relationship with Him. If we're ever going to overcome our idols, we must have a living relationship with the God who is greater than all gods.

We started off this book with Psalm 135:5: "I know that the LORD is great, that our Lord is greater than all gods" (NIV). We've journeyed together through a process of discovery, led by the Holy Spirit, and now it's important for us to lay aside every idol. Remember that replacing our idols is just as critical as removing them if we are to walk in lasting freedom. God doesn't just tell us to avoid idol worship. His hope is that we would love Him so much that we wouldn't be tempted with idolatry at all. In order to steer clear of idols that will return us to a life of slavery, we need to keep a few things in mind.

It's always more comfortable to drift back to old patterns than to create new ones. This is why a lot of people see initial results with a diet but can't stick with it for long. Those old habits want to be resurrected, but we need to give it time and keep plugging away at establishing new habits. It's also why people text their ex when it's late at night. It's easy to forget how bad it was when they were in that relationship. It's better to be alone with God than to be in a bad relationship that's only going to drag you down, but we tend to remember the good stuff and forget the bad. Life is hard, and it's time to choose our hard. Being on a diet is hard, but so is being overweight. Being alone is hard, but so is being in a bad relationship. Choose the "hard" that will make your life better.

We naturally gravitate toward comfort, not calling. We want to take the easy way and not go the Lord's way. When God told Ananias to help Paul (Acts 9), it would have been easier for Ananias to say, "Hold on a minute, Lord. I know that You need someone to go and restore Paul's sight, but let me get an older Christian in his nineties who doesn't have as much to lose as I do. I'll be back in five." But that's not what happened.

Until this time, Paul was a threat to the church and would have been an enemy to Ananias, who chose to obey at the cost of his own safety. The Lord's way takes dedication and daily submission, so Ananias was committed to obeying God despite the risk!

Think of a healthy marriage relationship: it takes commitment. When we said our vows on our wedding day, we might have promised, "In sickness and in health, for richer, for poorer, till death do us part." It's easy to say those words on that day, because we are in love and everyone is healthy. The vows w take on our wedding day aren't for that day but for when sickness comes, we lose our jobs, we bury our loved ones, and life gets real. To keep our marriage healthy, we choose to honor that commitment through the storms of life. God wants us to stay faithfully committed to Him during the storms, too.

The culture we live in and the issues we face will never make it easy to live free from idols. This is the same problem the Corinthian church faced. They asked about how to stay away from idolatry in a culture inundated with idols. Paul addressed this issue in his letter to them:

Now about food sacrificed to idols: We know that "We all possess knowledge." But knowledge puffs up while love builds up. Those who think they know something do not yet know as they ought to know. But whoever loves God is known by God.

So then, about eating food sacrificed to idols: We know that "An idol is nothing at all in the world" and that "There is no God but one." For even if there are so-called gods, whether in heaven or on earth (as indeed there are many "gods" and many "lords"), yet for us there is but one God, the Father, from whom all things came and for whom we live; and there is but one Lord, Jesus Christ, through whom all things came and through whom we live.

But not everyone possesses this knowledge.
—1 Corinthians 8:1–7 (NIV)

What you know isn't as important as how well you love. Notice the repeated use of the word *know* in this passage. When a word appears in Scripture that many times, it's important to pay attention. Also, take note of what is said about knowledge puffing up and love building up. When we show love to others, they are built up and encouraged. Our knowledge can easily become another idol we use to impress others, but people are probably more irritated by our arrogance than impressed by what we have to say.

God doesn't want us to be puffed up with information. He wants us to know the truth about ourselves, and He wants us to love in a way that bears all things. Loving God first and loving people second is the greatest way to keep ourselves on track.

Another thing the passage above tells us is that real love and true freedom are found only in knowing Jesus Christ. You might have heard about Him and heard stories of His power, but do you really know Him on a personal level? It's easy to feel as if we know some of our favorite celebrities because we've seen them in movies and on television, but if we were ever in the same room with them, someone would have to introduce us. We know of them. We know things about them. But we don't really know them.

Many of us view God in the same way. Maybe we went to Sunday school and learned the story of Adam and Eve and the forbidden fruit. Maybe we know that Christmas is a celebration of when Jesus was born. Maybe we know that Easter is not just about eggs and bunnies; it's about Jesus being crucified for our sins and raised from the dead. These statements are fine and good, but what are we doing in response to all of this intellectual knowledge? What does the way we live say about what's truly reigning in our hearts?

Perhaps you go to church on Sunday and put some change in the offering basket, but does God really know you? King David said, "I know that the LORD is great" (Psalm 135:5 NIV). David knew God on a close personal level. The worst way some of us can be deceived is thinking that we are right with God because we know some basic facts about Jesus and have read stories about Him. Jesus warned us about this in Matthew 7:21–24 (NIV):

> Not everyone who says to me, "Lord, Lord," will enter the kingdom of heaven, but only the one who does the will of my Father who is in heaven. Many will say to me on that day, "Lord, Lord, did we not prophesy in your name and in your name drive out demons and in your name perform many miracles?" Then I will tell them plainly, "I never knew you. Away from me, you evildoers!"
>
> Therefore everyone who hears these words of mine and puts them into practice is like a wise man who built his house on the rock.

Being close to God means that we're listening intimately to Him and obeying Him. This personal relationship with God is what will bring peace, purpose, and direction to our hearts and lives. The word translated as *know* is the Greek word *ginōskō*, which means to know, to come to know, to get a knowledge of, or to perceive or feel.[16] Knowing God is much deeper than head knowledge. Our hearts must be committed to Him if we are truly to know Him.

Idol worship ends where a clean heart and an intimate relationship with God begin. Knowing Jesus intimately means choosing Him every single day of our lives. It means laying down our own rights, our wants, our wishes, and our idols to follow Him and what He wants. Living this way is how we build our lives on solid ground.

God loves us and has an amazing plan for each of our lives. When we stop settling for unworthy things, we can finally love Him and worship Him with all we are and all we have. Only then will we truly see that our God is *Greater Than* anything this world has to offer!

REFERENCES

Notes

1. *Englishman's Greek Concordance of the New Testament,* "resist." By George Wigram. Hendrickson, 1996.

2. *Brown-Driver-Briggs Hebrew and English Lexicon,* "'ābad." By Francis Brown, Samuel Rolles Driver, and Charles Augustus Briggs.

3. Hess, Jared. *Napoleon Dynamite.* Fox Searchlight Pictures / Paramount Pictures, 2004.

4. Wiedeman, Reeves. "Dealing with Olympic Failure." *The New Yorker.* July 23, 2012. https://www.newyorker.com/sports/sporting-scene/dealing-with-olympic-failure.

5 . Josephus, Flavius. *Antiquities of the Jews* 8.15.5.

6. Groeschel, Craig. "Defeating the Four Enemies of Growth, Part

1." *Craig Groeschel Leadership Podcast*. https://podcasts.apple.com/us/podcast/craig-groeschel-leadership-podcast/id1070649025?i=1000487291862.

7. Keller, Timothy. *Counterfeit Gods: The Empty Promises of Money, Sex, and Power, and the Only Hope That Matters*. Penguin Publishing Group, 2011, p. 45.

8. *Old Testament Hebrew Lexical Dictionary*, "Strong's #3747 – כְּרִית." StudyLight.org. https://www.studylight.org/lexicons/eng/hebrew/3747.html.

9. Wooden, John, and Steve Jamison. *A Lifetime of Observations and Reflection On and Off the Court*. McGraw-Hill, 1997.

10. Blue Letter Bible, "Strong's H1008 – *bêṯ-'ēl*." https://www.blueletterbible.org/lexicon/h1008/kjv/wlc/0-1/.

11. *Old & New Testament Greek Lexical Dictionary*, "Strong's #278 – ἀμεταμέλητος." StudyLight.org. https://www.studylight.org/lexicons/eng/greek/278.html.

12. Tozer, A. W. *Man: The Dwelling Place of God*. Christian Publications, 1990.

13. Keller, Timothy. "If your God never disagrees with you...." Twitter post, 12:00 p.m., September 12, 2014. https://twitter.com/timkellernyc/status/510458013606739968?lang=en.

14. Beall, A., Molieri, F., dir. *Happines Is a Warm Blanket, Charlie Brown*. Warner Bros. Television Distribution, 2011.

15. *A Greek–English Lexicon* (Liddell–Scott–Jones), "θαρσέω." By Henry George Liddell, Robert Scott, and Henry Stuart Jones. 1843. In "Strong's #2293," StudyLight.org.

https://www.studylight.org/lexicons/eng/greek/2293.html.

16. Bible Study Tools, "ginosko." https://www.biblestudytools.com/lexicons/greek/nas/ginosko.htm.

About the Author

Tim Ingram is the lead pastor of HighRidge Church Longview, a growing, thriving community of Christ-followers who are passionate about taking faith steps, seeing lives change, and adding value to their community.

In addition to providing leadership and vision for HighRidge, Tim is also the president of Unite Leadership, whose purpose is to train and equip church and business leaders to make an impact in their local community.

Tim is a skilled communicator specializing in the areas of healthy leadership, spiritual growth, and transforming culture. His energetic, humorous, and refreshingly honest approach to teaching deep biblical truths with practical, everyday application is truly unique.

An avid outdoorsman and Dallas Cowboys fan, Tim resides in the beautiful Piney Woods of East Texas with his wife Tina, their young adult children T.J. and Natalie, and their dog Leia.

About Renown Publishing

Renown Publishing was founded with one mission in mind: to make your great idea famous.

At Renown Publishing, we don't just publish. We work hard to pair strategy with innovative marketing techniques so that your book launch is the start of something bigger.

Learn more at RenownPublishing.com.

Made in USA - North Chelmsford, MA
1300373_9781952602634
01.25.2022 1558